W9-DCH-548

SAVANNAH
HAUNTINGS!
A Walking Tourist Guidebook

by

ROBERT EDGERLY

Copyright © 2005 by Robert Edgerly

All rights reserved. No part of this book may be reproduced or utilized in any form or by any means, electronic or mechanical, including photocopying, recording or by any information storage and retrieval system, without prior permission from the Publisher. Inquiries should be addressed to:

See Savannah Books
P. O. Box 10903
Savannah, GA 31412
(912) 441-9277
www.seesavannah.com

Photos courtesy of Georgia Historical Society

ISBN 978-1-57087-749-0
Library of Congress Control Number 2006932853

Second Edition, 2006
Third Edition, 2008
Fourth Edition, 2009
Printed in the USA

CONTENTS

INTRODUCTION

Strange. Savannah is strange. That fact quickly became clear to me when I moved to the city in 1990. Draped with Spanish moss and populated with some real characters, the Historic District in those days exuded what appeared to be a native weirdness. The strange I was becoming aware of went deeper than that.

Savannah may not be the most haunted city in the nation; I don't know how to judge that, but anecdotal evidence heavily supports a profusion of hauntings. Everybody has a ghost story. Anybody who has lived in downtown Savannah for any length of time has a personal ghost story. They can relate an actual personal experience with a ghost. They have felt something or seen something or experienced something that made neck hair stand to attention. Everybody is a pretty good portion of a population to be relating so many similar stories if there is not something actually happening.

Robert Edgerly, a veteran tour operator and connoisseur of good stories, has collected some of the best hauntings stories in this book. Even more delightful, he has put these tales in historical and social context.

To orient the self-guided walking tourist Robert has included a map keyed to the various stories in the book. The number on the map corresponds to a page number in the book. A listing of these subjects is provided for easy reference.

HAUNTINGS !

The book is also a perfect companion to Robert's Hauntings Tour. Most of the stories in the book are told in the course of the leisurely evening stroll through the heart of the Historic District and many locations are visited. The tours depart from 135 Bull Street at 7 and 9 pm all year. Cameras are welcome. You may get a photo of something different.

The book focuses on some of the most popular stories but the visitor should realize that there is much more to discover. These stories are only the tip of the iceberg.

Savannah is strange.

— Jess C. Henderson

THOUGHTS

The ghost story is the oldest type of supernatural tale, and thus the one closest to the oral storytelling tradition. It is meant to be brief, the better to deliver its thrills to captivated listeners before the tenuous air of suspense has time to dissipate.

> *"Gave a man a turn it did, it was something queer, you kind of felt cold and thin in your very marrow, it went down my spine like ice.'"*
> H.G. Wells

> *"Just as it is possible to be scared by what you don't see, so it is possible to be haunted long after the briefest of encounters with the supernatural."*
> Stephen Dziemianowicz 1993

Fear comes in all shapes and sizes; these ghosts no matter how small will loom large in your memory.

PREFACE

Hauntings are universal. Every city has its own stories of phantoms and psychic phenomena, but in this respect Savannah is a special case. Savannah is not so much a place as it is a state of mind—a state of mind that lives in a romantic world, non-existent in many other parts of the country, but still preserved in the older sections of the city.

The city's slower, more tradition bound atmosphere tends to encourage a preoccupation with the occult. People in this area enjoy the fact that so many unexplained phenomena are in their midst. Many have a respect for the occult that make them more receptive to reports of occurrences of paranormal activity. It may have something to do with Savannah's physical location: an extinct barrier island left thirteen miles inland when the ocean levels dropped 12,000 years ago. It certainly has a lot to do with the people who inhabited this bluff on the Savannah River. Native Americans, Spanish, Scots, Irish, English, French, and Dutch, as well as the Portuguese and Austrians, with more coming through the years. The atmosphere for hauntings, ghosts, psychic activity, and astral phenomena is far more open in Savannah than in other cities. The early inhabitants are people of Anglo-Saxon origin and the Celtic heritage still permeates.

Our interest in the occult may have something to do with the ebb and flow of the tidal low country. Huge stands of live oaks, hung with funereal Spanish moss, holding firm to the loamy, sandy soil of the high ground. Magnolias shading mysterious haunts. Eerie imaginings of things past tend to occur in the twilight, not in the bright sunlight.

Then there is our architecture, from the colonial clapboards surrounding Trustees Garden on the east end of the bluff to the Georgian and Regency mansions sitting prettily on the many squares. Structures steeped in a colorful, sad, and often violent history. It is hardly surprising to discover that among the environs of Savannah many ghostly visitations and unexplained events are common. Savannah, with its old world charm and romantic settings, is particularly prone to hauntings.

The hauntings of Savannah are neither legendary nor figments of the imagination. They are the restless spirits of normal people who lived out their lives but died in distress or longing. Just as it is possible to be scared by what you don't see, so it is possible to be haunted long after by encounters with the supernatural.

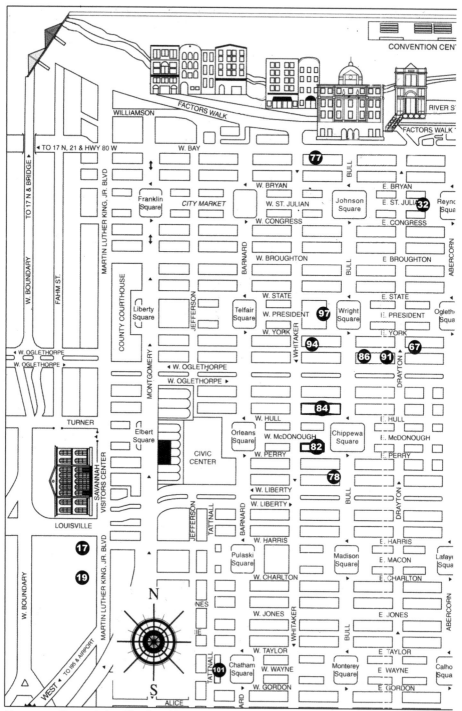

Map courtesy Savannah Area Chamber of Commerce

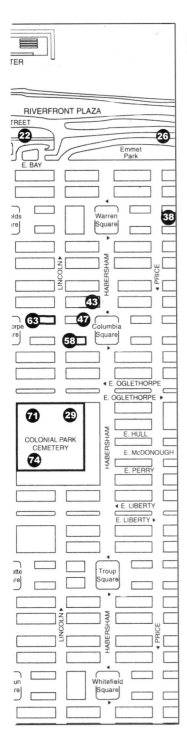

WALKING ON THE DEAD

If you are in the Historic District of Savannah, chances are good that you're standing or walking on the dead. Many burial grounds are spread under the city. The original city is uniformly about a mile wide and approximately ten miles long. It runs between the bluffs of two rivers: Yamacraw Bluff on the Savannah River (where River Street is today), to Coffee Bluff on the Forest River, ten miles south. General Oglethorpe, the founder of the colony, would have ridden between these two bluffs many times. The first road in the village was called White Bluff Road until a portion was renamed in honor of Colonel William Bull. Oglethorpe and Bull laid out the road; it cuts the high ground of Savannah right down the middle, lengthwise.

The Native Americans who were here when the colonists arrived were members of the Creek-Choctaw nation and called themselves Guale (pronounced Wally). Like the Choctaw, they lived in a necropolis, a city of the dead. They buried their dead above ground in mounds; the higher up the social strata, the higher up the mound you were planted. The natives lived around these mounds for thousands of years. Three of the largest burial mounds on the east coast used to be located up river at Port Wentworth, the Irene mounds. The site of the State Port Authority today, one was taken out by a flood in the early 1920's. Samuel Elbert's coffin was unearthed and found sticking out on the riverside of the mound. Found by some teenagers, he was reinterred in Colonial Park along with his wife, who was found next to him.

The second bloodiest battle of the War of Independence was fought in Savannah, the Siege and Battle of Savannah. It was a British victory, which is why most people have never heard of the battle. October 9, 1779, in 55 minutes, 1150 men died. If you watched a movie that had that much death in less than an hour, you would think it was exaggerated, but that's what happened here in 1779. It was a massacre by today's standards; only 150 British were killed, over 1000 allies were killed.

At the corner of Bull and York Streets at Wright Square affixed to the wall of one of the storefronts is a cast iron plaque. It explains that the entire block bounded by Bull, York, Whitaker and Oglethorpe was the city's first burial ground. Under these buildings and sidewalks and extending out under the Federal building are the remains of the first colonists. This was the Christian burial ground, and it filled up fast with fever victims. The settlement needed a new burial area so they incorporated the old Christ Church Cemetery, and enlarged it three times. That became Colonial Park Cemetery.

The first Jewish cemetery was located at Bull and South Broad (now Oglethorpe Ave.) and a granite marker in the west median explains that fact. Sixteen names, just a fraction of the names of the people interred here.

The original colonists landed in February of 1733, but by July of that year, 35 of the 114 colonists were dead and in the burial ground. That same month a boatload of Portuguese Jews landed. Luckily for the colonists, Dr. Samuel Nunez, one of the most educated physicians of the day, stepped ashore. He was immediately put to work by Oglethorpe to stem the tide of deaths. Nunez told the founder that he didn't know what caused the fever but he thought he could bring it under control. He did just that, by wrapping the victims in wet blankets and, with the use of quinine, he was able to stop the epidemic. Oglethorpe gave the Jewish settlers refuge and they became the third oldest Jewish congregation in the country possessing the oldest Torah in North America.

The southern expansion of the city limits caused the Jews to open a new cemetery west of there, and in 1818 the Presbyterian Church was built on the southern side of South Broad Street (now Oglethorpe) at Bull. Permission was given by Mickve Israel Synagogue to build the church over the old burials. Over the front door of the church is a Latin prayer to the Father, Son and the Holy Spirit. There is also an inscription honoring Jehovah, God of the Jews, because the presbyters knew they were building on the Jewish dead.

The second Jewish burial ground is located further west at 1-16 and Cohen Street. Surrounded by a brick wall, it is only used by descendants of the people buried there. When the city opened Laurel Grove and Bonaventure cemeteries, the Jews began interring their loved ones there.

The second Christian burial ground for the city, Colonial Park Cemetery, was known most of its life as the Old Brick Burial Ground or the Brick Wall Cemetery. Until 1896, a seven-foot tall, two-foot wide brick wall stood around the perimeter. It went out over the present day sidewalk on the Abercorn Street side. When the wall was removed, the west perimeter was brought in so as to add the sidewalk. The markers laying to the left as you walk into the cemetery today are very easily discernible on the old Christ Church maps. Also underneath the entrance at the corner of Abercorn Street and Oglethorpe Avenue is a family vault. The Daughters of the American Revolution installed the gate in 1913. There was a vault in the corner at that time so its roof was removed and the entrance gate erected. The vault is still there. Simply by entering the cemetery through its main gate you are treading on the dead.

There are other areas in this city used as burial grounds that are now under our buildings, squares, and streets. The 'stranger's plot' or 'potter's field' was for burials of those with no connections to Savannahians. It was located from Taylor Street to Gordon Street at Abercorn, under what is now the Massie School and Calhoun Square. The Negro and slave cemetery was adjacent to potter's field and extended as far south as Huntingdon Street at Abercorn, now under homes and streets, many of which have a history of haunting.

There are many burials spread all around downtown Savannah for various reasons. One reason courtyards, gardens and basements in the city are set with tombstones is because people are buried throughout Historic District residents' yards. During the Federal occupation by Union troops part of the Catholic Cemetery was dug up. The Confederates already had earthworks set on the east end of the bluff covering the city in case of attack from down river (sand-traps at the Savannah Golf Club are Confederate earthworks built in 1860). The Union troops began enlarging the earthworks to the south and dug up bodies. A bishop and two priests as well as several others were excavated. The Catholic hierarchy got involved and General Gilmer, whom General Sherman had left in charge of the city, was threatened with excommunication (he was a devout Catholic) by the bishop of New York City. In the meantime the local priests were instructing their parishioners to retrieve their loved ones. Consequently many Catholics were dug up and moved to safer ground. They were re-interred in their family yards with the thought of temporarily storing them. Many were returned but some were left where they lay, a third burial being too inconvenient or maybe it was a case of merely being more comfortable closer to home.

The Sisters of Mercy dug up twenty nuns who had been buried over the years in the Catholic Cemetery, put all of their remains in a single coffin and re-buried it in the grotto in the courtyard of their convent. Those nuns are still there to this day.

DEVASTATING FIRES

Savannah has burned four times in her history. Just like any other city her size and age, Savannah has had many major fires, but on four occasions over half the city has burned and all four fires started in the same area.

The fire of November 26th, 1796 started in the bake house of Mr. Grommet in Market Square, destroying nearly every house between Barnard and Abercorn Streets, from Bay to Broughton. A total of 229 houses were destroyed in four hours, four hundred families were left homeless, and many dead.

January 11th, 1820—A terrible fire burning 463 houses, with the exception of the Planter's Bank (known today as the Pink House), Christ Church, and three or four brick buildings. Every building north of Broughton Street was destroyed. The fire continued from one in the morning on Tuesday to one o'clock Wednesday afternoon. Hundreds were killed.

January 27th, 1865, the day Sherman's army crossed the river to South Carolina. Fire began in the stable of Granite Hall, corner of West Broad and Zubly Streets, and destroyed over 100 buildings. Several thousand rounds of ammunition stored in Granite Hall were ignited, and the explosion killed one and wounded three, adding terror to the occasion.

April 6th, 1889—Fire started in the store of D. Hogan, on the corner of Barnard and Broughton Streets. Independent Presbyterian Church, Guard's

Armory, and Odd Fellows Hall, along with many other buildings, were destroyed, and dozens were killed. Three of these fires started at City Market; today housing art galleries and restaurants. The City Market is located on the two northwestern most squares, Franklin Square and Ellis Square. Savannah is on a forty foot bluff surrounded by low country marsh and prevalent westerly winds. All three fires began when the wind was blowing hard from the west and then blew east destroying most of the city.

The historic district today is a 19th and 20th century city because the 18th century town is gone. There are a handful of 18th century buildings; most are located near the Pirate's House Restaurant on the east end of the bluff on East Broad Street across from the Mulberry Inn. By the time the fires moved east the wind played out, the fire changed course and some were spared.

Savannah is a brick and mortar city today because of the fires and the eclectic mix of architecture is due to the fact that three to four times the city had to be rebuilt. There are several "fire-proof" buildings in Savannah: the U.S. Customs House, The Independent Presbyterian Church and the Kehoe house, just to name a few.

YELLOW FEVER, BLACK DEATH

Yellow Fever plagued Savannah from her very beginning. Every year logged dozens of deaths, some years hundreds, but three epidemics caused thousands of deaths. At the south end of Colonial Cemetery are mass burials with hundreds of bodies. In 1820, 1854 and again in 1876, three horrible yellow fever epidemics struck the area and thousands died.

In 1820, Savannah was a small village of 6,000 people averaging 10 deaths a day. Gravediggers couldn't keep up, and on some occasions dug pits and covered the bodies with sand between loads. Half the population was gone; the other half was locked in their homes. The only people on the streets were the highly paid men who drove the death wagons. They didn't so much as drive them but walk beside them and load the bodies; the mules knew where to go because of having to make the trip to the cemetery day after day.

Anywhere you travel along the east or gulf coast, turn inland, travel about two hours, and you will find small towns with avenues of live oaks and magnolias. These are the fever-season cities built by the landed gentry, the planter aristocrats. Every July they would pack their children and their slaves and move inland not to return until October. They didn't know that the first freeze killed the mosquito larvae; they just knew they could start coming back in October.

Residents thought the dirt of the streets caused yellow fever. They thought the fog that rolls in July and August caused it. Some residents believed an effluvial miasma from the cemetery brought the deaths. They didn't realize that mosquitoes in their backyard were killing them, and as a double onus for Savannah, rice plantations: aqua culture and a prime habitat for mosquitoes surrounded the town.

The people of Savannah thought yellow fever was contagious; it isn't. Today we know that mosquitoes carry yellow fever. The bacterium has been eradicated in this hemisphere but the mosquitoes still exist. The fever was seasonal, lasting from July through October, so people could plan for it, so to speak.

Yellow fever is a horrible way to die; the young and elderly go first. The kidney and liver shuts down, and the victim turns yellow, hence the name. Later the patient turns black, swells up, and it can take weeks before death. It sounds horrendous today, but when a family member died, the body would be set out on the stoop and they would shut the door. The death wagons would come around and collect the bodies. So during these epidemics, the streets were figuratively and literally littered with bodies. (It was not a good idea to take a nap on the front porch).

It wasn't until Dr. Walter Reed figured out, when the Panama Canal was being built, that mosquitoes carried the deadly fever; before that, people didn't have a clue. This also led to many people being pronounced dead who weren't. Yellow fever attacks the respiratory system and victims went into comas. The families and city health workers didn't know they were still alive and many were buried alive. That is why people used a mirror to check for any telltale breath from victims. It is also the reason alarm systems were developed to safe guard against mistakenly burying the living.

We use terms in our lexicon everyday in this country that come from living with death. We don't know the origins of these terms because we don't live with death like we used to or like people in other parts of the world still do. Today when someone dies, the next time we see him or her, they are displayed in a coffin and look very nice; we put them in a crypt or take the remains home in an urn.

In the past, the family handled the dead; it was an age-old custom. There was a door in the house that came easily off the hinges just for the purpose of laying out the dead. The deceased would be laid out for a short time, then wrapped in a shroud and buried quickly, especially in the South, for obvious reasons. People had a great fear of being buried alive in the pre-Victorian era before the advent of embalming. Many went to elaborate schemes and designs to prevent such occurrences:

Morticians installed vent pipes in the burial vault with a chain connected to a bell. When laid on the shelf of the vault a silk string would be tied to the wrist of the deceased and attached to the bell. If revived, by flaying one's arms around he or she would be 'saved by the bell'. Someone had to be at his post in the cemetery to hear the bell, giving rise to the 'graveyard shift'.

How about a 'dead ringer'? That's when you walk down the street one day and turn the corner and before you stands a man whose funeral was the month before. You run up to him and grab him by the collar and say, "I thought we put you in the crypt," and he says, "Yes, but I'm a dead ringer!"

SPANISH MOSS

Funereal Spanish moss hangs from the live oaks, the magnolias, dogwoods, and seems to choke the crepe myrtle. You notice the Spanish moss as you walk or drive through Savannah. The city is full of it. It's an epiphyte, an air plant, actually a member of the bromeliad family. Moss doesn't harm the plant that hosts it. It gets its nutrients from the air and water that filters through the trees. Moss doesn't like pine trees. It doesn't like magnolia trees except for a couple that I know of that are growing on haunted sites. Moss won't grow in a palmetto tree, but it loves oak trees, and the squares and other green spaces are covered with it.

One of the legends of how it gets its name is from the Spanish conquistadors, who came through here in the 1500's and 1600's. Not particularly pleasant fellas; they wore armor, carried flintlock weapons and looked like something from outer space to the natives who lived here. Conquistadors kidnapped, tortured and killed natives by the hundreds in their quest for gold.

The legend goes that one of the conquistadors was betrothed to a native princess and after the marriage ceremony he went to the matrimonial dwelling to be with his bride, but she escaped out the back. She began running through the woods, jumping from tree limb to tree limb. He started chasing her and he continues to chase her to this day. Long tufts of his gray beard get blown through the oak trees, and that's the Spanish moss you see today all over Savannah.

Another Deep South legend tells of a romance of long ago...

A lovely princess and her love, upon their
 wedding day,
Were struck-down by a savage foe amidst a
 bitter fray;
United in death they were buried, so the
 legends go—
'Neath an oak's strong, friendly arms,
 protected from their foe;
There, as was the custom, they cut the
 bride's long hair with love
And hung its shining blackness on the
 spreading oak above;
Untouched, undisturbed it hung there, for all
 the world to see
And with the years the locks turned gray
 and spread from tree to tree.

TUNNELS

Savannah's historic district is built on an antebellum storm drain system that was installed under the streets in the 1850's. Slave labor was used to dig up the center of the avenues and brick drainage was installed. Brick walls eighteen inches thick, with a forty-eight inch opening, drained the sewerage and storm water into the river. Actually, many parts of the system acted as a sump holding sewerage until the next storm would flush it out. On each ramp that leads down to River Street, large openings can be seen in the bulkhead; storm water would flow right down the ramp carrying with it the city's sewerage.

A series of tunnels existed long before this system was built. These tunnels were first built by the Guale Indians who lived on this bluff for 15,000 years before the arrival of Europeans. Pirates, smugglers and native traders used these tunnels to store contraband from the Spanish and English authorities. Many tunnels extend to buildings on the bluff. Churchill's Pub on Bay Street and the Pirate's House at East Broad and Bay are just two of many buildings with tunnels. The "Sons of Liberty" or "Liberty Boys" used the tunnels until 1782, during British occupation of the city. Descendants of the original families used the tunnels again during the "War of Northern Aggression."

After the Stono rebellion in South Carolina—in which rebellious slaves massacred hundreds of plantation owners and their families in the 1820's— escape tunnels were installed in many homes in Savannah, built by slaves who were brought from the inland plantations to perform the work. The most extensive use of these underground passages was during the yellow fever epidemics. Contrary to some reports the dead were not carried through the tunnels; the living used the passages to get around the city. One such tunnel was discovered recently under Bull Street near the Sorrell-Weed House. The present owner discovered it when excavating the floor of the basement during a major renovation.

The men who ran the city used the tunnels. Candler Hospital and Telfair Hospital, at opposite ends of Forsyth Park, are connected with an underground passage. The jail, courthouse, and customs house were all connected underground.

After the epidemics, city council members voted funds to shore up the existing tunnels and to build additional passageways as needed. The men who ran the town would be able to go from building to building without having to be on the same streets as carts laden with yellow fever victims. So the living used the tunnels, while the epidemic raged on the streets above. During the epidemics half the population evacuated and the other half stayed shut up in their homes. Someone had to stay behind and run things, so to insure against contracting the fever, judges, doctors, city officials and ordinary citizens used the tunnels to move about and avoid the death above.

The Pulaski House Hotel (today a bank) stood on Johnson Square and the original two-level basement still exists. Tunnels lead from it to the river and to the

HAUNTINGS!

Old City Hotel (today Moon River Brewing Co.) on West Bay Street. There are many passages in the City Market area and most lead to the bluff. Even during Prohibition, liquor was stored and transported by way of the tunnels. The basement of the Marshall House Hotel on Broughton Street was a speak-easy and several tunnels led to other establishments of like atmosphere.

There are many hauntings below Savannah. The most famous is the area under Trustee's Garden where the Pirate's House restaurant is located today. There are at least four tunnels under the complex; two leading from the rum cellar located under the oldest of the buildings, the other two running under what was at one time the garden, today the "Buccaneer Room." The longest tunnel starts at the garden and runs north and south about seventy-five feet from the opening, which was discovered in the 1960's. An opening heads west and that tunnel is now sealed.

An inquisitive local historian decided to do a little spelunking. He got permission from the owner of the restaurant and went below to explore. As the historian was making his way along the passage he heard voices behind him. Glancing back, he saw two men dressed as seamen of the 18th century dragging an unconscious man, about to bear down on him. He jumped to the side and felt a cold blast of air as he watched, mesmerized, the three men walk right through the rubble of the sealed passage, oblivious to the fact he was there. He left the tunnel as quickly as he could and said he had no intention of ever returning.

The Battle of Savannah, the second bloodiest battle of the Revolutionary War, was fought in the Historic District. Eight o'clock in the morning of October 9th, 1779, eleven hundred fifty men were killed in 55 minutes. A remarkable amount of carnage, but that's what happened south and west of downtown at Springhill Redoubt (today the Savannah Visitors Center and Roundhouse Railroad Museum). The British casualties totaled 150 men. They had leisure to bury their dead and moved them to Beaufort SC, to what became the National Cemetery (they are in a corner of that cemetery today). The allies did not have that leisure. They were given twenty-four hours to get out of town, and under a flag of truce they left behind Haitian regiments to bury their dead. From Madison Square west are dozens of bodies and as you move west tens of dozens. Underneath the Visitors Center is a mass grave, with hundreds of patriots who died for our liberty.

In Madison Square stands a bronze statue of one of the battle's heroes. There are hundreds of bronze statues in this country but only two of this type: this one, of a noncommissioned officer, Sergeant William Jasper; the other is the flag raising at Iwo Jima, also non-comms. Sergeant Jasper is shown as he was mortally wounded recovering the colors of his home state,

South Carolina. He, too, is buried in the mass grave under the Savannah Visitors Center.

In Monterey Square is a beautiful Beaux Arts masterpiece, a memorial to Count Casimir Pulaski, the first allied general to die in battle. He was known as the father of the U.S. Calvary and he was killed in the Battle of Savannah.

The carnage was horrific and a sense of gloom still permeates the air in this area. The sounds of bagpipes can be heard to this day in the vicinity of Louisville Road and Martin Luther King, Jr. Boulevard during the month of October. The eerie sounds of the pipes mournfully remind us of the tragedy long ago.

THE LATHE

There can be many different types of hauntings and some do not involve noise, odor or a sighting. One in particular that comes to mind happened back in the mid 1990's at the Georgia State Railroad Museum. I had the distinct pleasure of being involved in the early stages of stabilization and restoration of the antebellum facility.

The site was designed and built in the 1840's and 1850's, with a few modernizations and enlargements in the 1920's. It operated as the maintenance shop for the Central of Georgia Railroad into the early 1970's. It is a fine example of pre-Civil War southern technology and a lasting tribute to the men who built and operated it.

When the City of Savannah asked the Coastal Heritage Society to step in and save the site from further decay, it had been sitting dormant and unoccupied for almost 20 years. Much damage was caused during the filming for the movie *Glory,* and because of the lack of maintenance the five-acre site was decaying rapidly.

The turntable was made operable and a fledgling blacksmith program was established in the maintenance shop. The railroad had literally scrapped every piece of equipment at the site and the bridge over Louisville Road had been removed by the state DOT, so everything had to be brought in and set up with the help of corporate sponsors, donations and acquisitions.

The C.H.S., with funding from the City of Savannah, implemented an aggressive program of finding and acquiring machinery and rolling stock from around the country. Talented volunteers and staff members spent countless hours bringing the site back to life. The whole site was steam powered, that is to say there was a main steam engine that ran a system of shafts throughout the shops which operated the machinery with pulleys and belt drives. Needless to add, this was archaic technology.

Many pieces were put together with the help of retired workers and employees who gave of their time to help rebuild the infrastructure so that some of the machinery was slowly reassembled and made operational. One piece was particularly daunting, a 25-foot long lathe. It was massive, and because of the determination of the Society's weapons expert and blacksmith, John Roberson, it was made to run. But not without some help.

John had begun to reassemble the lathe but about halfway through became a little confused as to the proper configuration of the many gears and pulleys used to turn the huge metal cutting device. One particular day after spending much frustrating time trying to figure it out, he threw up his arms and said, "That's it, I can't go any further. It just doesn't seem to make sense to me."

We all went to lunch and left a young lady on the site in the gift shop admission booth. While we were gone, a funny thing happened: a woman came in with a stack of books and manuals to donate. The Society has a lot of paperwork to complete for proper cataloging and documentation of donations and the young lady tried to explain this to the woman. The woman said she had been carrying this stuff around in the trunk of her car for months and had promised her deceased father—who had retired after 40 years of service at this very shop complex—that she would bring it to the roundhouse and see to it that we took possession.

She said she didn't care to fill out any paperwork and just left the stack of manuals on the counter and walked out. About ten minutes later we all came back from our lunch break and John immediately noticed the pile of books. Being a conservationist, he quickly realized these were manuals for assembling and operation of metalworking machinery. John went through the stack and opened one book in particular and looked at the crew and said, "Guys, you're not going to believe this, but here is the lathe and this is how it is put together." We all looked up astonished and he proceeded to point out in the pages the proper way to assemble that particular 25-foot lathe.

Now you can call that a coincidence if you like, but I believe something else was at work here. A lot of blood, sweat and tears went into the daily operation of the nearly 150-year-old site and there were a lot of forces at work trying to bring it back to its former days of glory. One of those forces was the woman's dead father who had spent most of his life working there.

EXCHANGE TAVERN

One of Savannah's oldest and favorite eating establishments, the Cotton Exchange Tavern on River Street has gone through its share of owners but the ghosts remain the same.

Jean, a bartender who has been on duty there for 24 years, told me how she has worked for different owners but throughout the years the paranormal activity has remained. One of the regular occurrences happens when the bar is full and noisy with patrons. On the west side of the horseshoe shaped bar, a beer bottle sitting in front of a thirsty customer will raise up three or four inches and spin or shake, the bottle then sets back down and tilts side to side. The movement is as if someone is toying with the customers.

One particular incident still raises the hair on Jean's neck. This was years ago, before the windows were cut into the twenty-four inch thick ballast stone to bring some light into the old cotton warehouse. There was an old brass beverage cooler on the back of the bar with two shelves to display the various brands of bottled beer sold. She walked in the front door and turned on the light behind the bar and watched in amazement as the glass door slid open and each beer on the top shelf one by one teetered right off onto the floor. The bottles on the bottom shelf took the domino effect and fell from left to right each hitting the other. Jean stood there in amazement as the door to the cooler slowly slid shut and then she high tailed it out of there.

Another time Craig, who has been there almost as long as Jean, was locking up and had gone upstairs to turn up the thermostat on the AC and turn off the lights. He had done this innumerable times, but this night was different. Craig had just reached the top of the stairs, as the hair on the back of his neck stood up and he felt a cold chill. He went to the thermostat and as he was adjusting the dial, he felt someone tapping him on the shoulder. He turned to see that no one was standing behind him. Craig said he bolted down the stairs in two leaps and was out the front door in a flash.

TABLE TWENTY

The Cotton Exchange Tavern has a long history; the building dates to the 1850's, and the first two floors are made of ballast stone and brick. The walls are twenty-four inches thick and the doors are old growth heart pine timbers. The whole of River Street was the port for the city up until World War I. After that period the port was moved upriver, today located above the city past the new Talmadge Bridge, which was built to accommodate the large container vessels that come and go.

Jake, one of the managers, had an encounter with one of the early inhabitants. The establishment opens for lunch around 11 a.m. and the staff starts arriving a couple of hours before to get set up and prepare for the day's business. Jake was the first to come in that day, and having unlocked the huge front doors, walked in to find that someone was sitting at table twenty.

At first he didn't notice the apparition because the table is located to the right of the front door as you walk in. He went around the back of the bar and began turning on the lights; that's when he noticed the ghost sitting in the booth. Jake said he watched as the specter got up from his seat and proceeded to walk into the adjacent dining area.

Needless to add, Jake was upset. He said the ghost was a shade, a translucent shape of a person, and he glided across the floor. Jake ran around from the bar area and peered into the dining area and saw no one.

He then saw an orb as big as a man drifting between the bar and the kitchen. He immediately walked out and locked the door and waited for some of the other staff to arrive. (It is important to add that there is no back door to the Cotton Exchange Tavern.)

After waiting for about ten minutes the cook and a waitress showed up. Jake told them what he had seen and they went in to investigate. They barred the door from the inside and proceeded to search the premises. There was no one in the restaurant but them!

HEADLESS JOE

Many of the slaves in Savannah worked a trade as blacksmith, brick mason or carpenter and some were given relative independence by their masters to work and live on their own. One such slave was Joe. He would do his work and give his master a percentage. He had a small shanty on the east side near the old rice fields and when he wasn't working he would spend most of his time down on the east end of the riverfront.

Joe's favorite pastime was fishing. He spent most of the time during the incoming tide fishing down by the walls of Fort Wayne at the east end of River Street. There were a lot of good-sized bass and mullet in the river and they could be caught right off the bulkhead. One day Joe had been catching quite a few fish. He draped them over the edge of the wharf, hanging from a small rope. Joe lay down to catch a nap and fell fast asleep.

The river rose until it reached the fish hanging over the side. About this time one of the large alligators that transit the river at high tide caught a scent of Joe's fish. The gator slowly came up and opened his great mouth. Joe's head was just inches from where the fish hung, and when the gator snapped his jaws shut, Joe's head disappeared with the fish!

Joe still hangs around the east end of the waterfront to this day; he's an angry haunt. He's angry because a gator took his mess of fish that he spent all afternoon catching and to beat it all, the gator took his head, too. Now his headless shape is seen quite often on the East Broad Street ramp, and especially on the stairs that lead up from the river. It seems that Joe is still searching for his catch and his head. Caution: one of Joe's favorite pranks is to trip you as you walk up the stairs!

SEA CABINS

The owners of Sails and Rails on River Street operate an inn upstairs on Factors Walk called the Sea Cabins. They are quite nice and have all that you need for a comfortable stay in Savannah. Just bring some groceries and you're set. The best part is the view: ships from all over the world pass by the window and the Historic District is at your doorstep.

The buildings are cotton warehouses that date from the late nineteenth century. There seems to be a mischievous presence in the Sea Cabins. The housekeepers will clean the suites between occupants and everything is left shipshape, so to speak. The owner will do a walk-through to ensure that everything is in order.

Sometimes guests will check in late and get their key from a lock box and settle in for the night. The next morning, the owner will ask if the room is to their satisfaction and the guests will say everything is fine, but why are there no light bulbs? This has been going on for years and no one seems to be able to explain it.

The only way the bulbs can be removed from the ceiling and the ceiling fans is with a ladder. There is no ladder in the suites, but the bulbs disappear into thin air. No one has access to the rooms between the time of inspection by the owner and the time guests check in and sometimes the time in between is less than an hour—*but the bulbs vanish!*

RENE'S PLAYGROUND

Rene Rondolia Asch grew up in the area known as the "Old Fort" (so named because it's the area on the northeast corner of the bluff around Fort Wayne). He was born large and grew to be much larger. Rene was seven feet tall and weighed more than 350 pounds; he was fourteen years old when he was lynched, just before the great fire of 1820.

Rene used to hang out in the Old Brick Cemetery, known as Colonial Park today. This was his playground; he would hang around the vaults and play.

Everyone was afraid of Rene. He was mentally slow and wallowed his hulk around the neighborhood. Those spotting him coming down the sidewalk would drag their families to the other side of the street. Rene would enter the cemetery and others would take the nearest exit. He had a penchant for killing small animals. It isn't known if he did it on purpose, but he would handle them so roughly that he crushed them. He kept a graveyard next to his house for his animal victims. He built small coffins for them and buried them with markers. The whole town was afraid of him and rightfully so.

One night, the firemen across the street from the Old Brick Cemetery noticed Rene lumber home from the north gate, not thinking anything was amiss: this was 'Rene's playground'. Later in the wee hours of the morning, upon entering the south gate, a constable found the body of a young girl. She was crushed and her neck was broken.

A mob of angry citizens went to Rene's house and found him asleep. His French-Huguenot parents convinced the crowd Rene couldn't have done it, he was asleep in his bed. The whole city was in an uproar over the killing. Within 48 hours an ordinance was passed by the city council and Rene's parents were forced to build a stockade for the boy. Before the week was out, a brick addition was begun on the side of the parent's house. Before it was completed however, another body was discovered in the cemetery — killed in the same manner.

Again a mob of angry citizens went to Rene's house. Again they found him asleep. This time they paid no heed to the parents' plea. They dragged Rene down to the eastern wharves (site of the Marriott Hotel today) and they lynched him. The family was not able to inter him in the Old Brick Cemetery because he was thought to be a killer; this was consecrated ground, the public burial ground, and there was no room for criminals. So the family paid the mortician to bury Rene east of town in the swamps of the old rice plantations, where the Savannah Golf Club is today. A vault was built with a ledger tablet just like the many table vaults in Colonial Cemetery, only much larger. During one of their regular visits to Rene's vault the Asch's found it open and empty. They never found Rene and they never found his coffin. A week later another body was found, killed in the same manner.

The whole city knew they had lynched the wrong man—or had they? For Rene still haunts the streets of the 'Old Fort' and hangs out in the cemetery long after dark when the fog is low. He's a vengeful poltergeist, vengeful for his wrongful death. He walks through the streets of the 'Old Fort' calling out his name—RENE!

If you grew up in the 'Old Fort' and your parents wanted you home before dark, they would tell you the story of Rene. I'm sure there were many old Irishmen who would stand in their backyards and yell, "RENE!"

THE PINK HOUSE

Located on Reynolds Square, the Pink House is the second oldest brick structure in Georgia. Built in 1771, the house was red brick with a white stucco finish. Over time the red from the brick leached through and the house acquired a pink hue. Today the house is painted the distinctive pink color.

James Habersham built the house in the Georgian style. His father, Joseph, was a staunch loyalist. James and his brother were 'Liberty Boys', members of the revolutionary movement. Their father coined the phrase, "Father against son, son against father," during the War of Independence.

The house is a restaurant today and one of the best taverns in the city is in the basement, the Planters Tavern. Patrons and staff of the restaurant see Major Habersham quite often in this house. The basement is also active with phenomena seemed to be caused by children, perhaps the offspring of the slaves who worked here through the generations.

I have a personal account from the house in the 1980's: I was having dinner on the second floor with my ex-wife, Paula. We were sitting at a window on the front left as you view the home from the street. I was facing the fireplace with my back to the stairway and the window on my left. We were having a glass of wine, waiting for our appetizer. Paula acknowledged someone over my right shoulder. I turned to see who was there and saw no one. I turned back to look at my wife. She was in a daze, her eyes staring away at nothing in particular, and she was blank faced as if she had seen a ghost!

I asked to whom she was speaking and she replied that he was a very charming man in a blue velvet swallowtail jacket and old-fashioned breeches. He was a handsome and very cultured gentleman and quite debonair. She then turned away and stared at the fire.

I asked the waiter if she had a man in period dress as a host or maitre d'. Instead of answering she said, "Please wait, I will be right back." She returned with the manager and we were asked to accompany him downstairs so that he could show us a portrait. We got to the first floor at the main entrance, where he pointed to the large framed painting hanging in the foyer. Paula turned to look and she fell back into my arms swooning.

A portrait of James Habersham stared back at us. Paula identified the man in the portrait as the 'pleasant gentleman' and apparently she was not the first to be charmed by the former resident. Major Habersham still takes pride in his home and enjoys the large crowds that visit each night--especially the ladies, it seems.

A student from the local art college worked there as a waitress and told me of her encounter. She said her boyfriend also worked in the restaurant as a busboy and they often pulled the same shifts. She recounted that one night after closing, the staff had finished cleaning and everyone was standing at the front door waiting for the tips to be shared out. She was standing in the foyer facing the maitre d' s desk and leaning on the column, telling of her visit to Tybee Island the weekend before. She had her back to the front door and was just talking away. Everyone was listening and she had their full attention. As she was speaking, she felt a hand on her shoulder but didn't bother to see who it was, thinking it was her beau joining in, so she just kept on talking.

The hand on her shoulder got heavier and she thought her boyfriend must be very tired because he kept pressing down more and more heavily. She came to the climax of her story when she turned to her boyfriend for acknowledgment and saw no one there. She fell to the floor on her knees crying hysterically.

I later spoke to the manager and she corroborated what the waitress had said because she witnessed the whole thing.

One of the most frequent phenomena occurs at closing. The staff has finished cleaning each dining room and the last chore involves snuffing the candles in the period sconces mounted on the walls. These are made of brass with a reflector plate to give off a surreal light around the room from the tapers.

The wait staff snuffs the candles, two in each dining room upstairs. The flame is extinguished *but the reflecting light remains.* Many times this happens. After snuffing the candles, the reflector plates still spread an unearthly light.

The original kitchen was in the basement and the servants also had quarters there. Today the Planter's Tavern inhabits the space where once so much household activity took place. The tavern, furnished as an English country pub, hosts a large central bar with a fire in each of the two hearths. A piano stands in the corner and local singer-songwriter Gail Thurmond is featured five nights a week.

Gail told me there are a number of slave children still living in the basement. She can see them flit from table to table out of the corner of her eye while she is playing. She told me of a child name Magumba who haunts the tavern. He has on occasion followed Gail home. He is very mischievous and plays pranks on the staff.

Other people who work there have told me the same thing. They will be working at a task, not consciously looking, and see movement with the periphery of their eye. When they look, there is nothing there. Most report the movement is low to the ground about the same height as the table and chairs.

Erica, one of the bartenders, has had many encounters with these mischievous pranksters over the years. She has noticed paranormal activity just about every night. The glasses seem to move just out of grasp when she reaches for them at busy times during her shift.

One night, I had a group upstairs for a private tour and while they finished their meal I was downstairs at the bar. It wasn't too busy that night and as I was waiting I struck up a conversation with a couple from NYC at the bar.

We talked about the many hauntings in Savannah when Erica came over to see how we were getting along. She explained how at times when she is busy moving from one side of the bar to the other taking orders and preparing drinks, she will get hit in the back of the head by a bottle of wine as it shoots out of the wooden rack above her head.

Right then, in front of us all, a wine bottle shot out of the rack and hit her like a projectile in the back of the head. Erica has waist length hair that she keeps in a bun on the back of her head and the floor behind the bar has a thick rubber mat. So there was no real damage to her or the bottle of wine. Erica just smiled and said, "See, it happens just like that."

When something falls it goes straight down, but this bottle was shot out of the overhead rack like it had been pushed. Erica, Gail, and the rest of the staff at the tavern seem to take it all in stride; the ghosts are just children, after all.

HAMPTON LILLIBRIDGE HOUSE

The most famous haunted house in the state of Georgia is the Hampton Lillibridge House in Savannah. Originally located on Bryan Street two blocks west of its present location, the three-story house is easily spotted because it features the only mansard styled gambrel roof in town. Built by Mr. Hampton of St. Simons Island in the 1790's as a townhouse for use when he was not at his plantation, his friend's wife died there right after the great fire of 1820, prompting Hampton to sell the house to a Mr. Lillibridge, who turned it into a boarding house.

We know of at least three deaths in the house. Mrs. Gould died of pneumonia in 1820; after it became a boarding house, a sailor hung himself from a four-poster bed on the top floor; and another sailor was killed with a knife during a card game on the second floor.

During an extensive renovation of the house in 1963, a major fault in the foundation caused the owner to have the house picked up and moved to a new location at 507 East St. Julian Street and set down atop a new foundation. The owner of the house was none other than antiques dealer Jim Williams, whose exploits are recorded in the book *Midnight in the Garden of Good and Evil.* The accounts of the Hampton Lillibridge House being haunted were first reported in the famous ghost seeker Hans Holzer's book, *The Phantoms of Dixie.* Holzer termed Jim "a man of impeccable judgment and taste," and researchers had concluded that a genuine psychic phenomenon was indeed taking place.

The home is one of a handful of structures to have survived the 1820 fire. In thirty-six hours of horror 463 buildings were burnt in a firestorm. One of the ghosts may very well be Mrs. Jane Harris Gould, who had come to Savannah for medical care and had to flee on a cold January night during the fire, contracted pneumonia, and died. She was dead before her husband arrived from St. Simons and was buried in Colonial Cemetery temporarily, with plans to be moved to the Gould plantation later. A hurricane coming on the heels of the fire that year made the move impossible.

After the devastation of the fire, hurricane, and yellow fever epidemic of 1820, the house changed hands and became a boarding house and sailors from all over the world stayed in its rooms but two seem to have never left. Not all of the occurrences are unpleasant; there is also a three-piece band that is heard playing in the house.

The doctor and his wife who live there now have heard the band playing Dixieland jazz.

The Hampton Lillibridge House stood next to a twin structure originally two blocks west and as it was being moved, its twin collapsed. One workman was killed and his death shook Jim up, even though he had done everything he could to reinforce the second house before the move. Jim had to go out of town on a buying trip and learned while he was away that the movers had found a tabby vault in the ground before placing the house on the new lot at St. Julian Street, and he told author Margaret DeBolt that he regretted not being there to investigate the vault.

Williams believed it was a crypt and told DeBolt that in the ghettos people couldn't afford fancy burials so they interred the dead in a common vault. Obviously, the vault on the site of the new location had been used many times because the house was so haunted. There are some who believe this was Rene Rondolia Asch's grave, but we'll never know who and how many may be buried there.

While Jim was out of town, he had two young men who lived across the street oversee the work that was being performed. Electricians and plumbers were hooking up the infrastructure of the residence. The building sat on timbers after the move and the brick masonry had not been replaced so there were no chimneys, just open holes where the fireplaces should have been. The men were enjoying a quiet Sunday at home when they heard the sound of music coming from the structure. They approached the house and could distinctly hear jazz music. There were no stairs, just a trap door with a padlock; they unlocked the hatch, set up a ladder and climbed into the parlor level. Each went looking for what they thought would be a boom box that had been left on by one of the workers. They searched the first floor, then walked upstairs and couldn't find the source of the music. As one waited the other went to the top floor to investigate. The music stopped; the first waited for the other to come back down from the top floor, but he never came. He walked up the stairs to find his friend on the wood floor face down with his fingernails dug into the floorboards.

The first man helped his friend to his feet and walked him downstairs. His friend was visibly shaken, and after throwing water in his face to make him coherent, he recounted the following: when he walked upstairs it felt like he had walked into a cool pool of water. It got quite cold and a sinister force tried to suck him down the open shaft of the chimney, so he threw himself to the floor and held on for dear life until his friend rescued him. They climbed down the ladder, locked the hatch, and as they were walking back to their apartment, the sound of jazz wafted from the direction of the house. Needless to add, neither went back to investigate.

Upon moving into the house, Jim was awakened the first night by the sound of someone walking on broken glass or sand next to his bed. He sat up and asked, "Who's there?" When he heard footsteps rush out of the room and down the hall, Jim jumped out of bed and ran into the hallway in time to see the door at the other end close. He ran to the door but it was locked. He found a key and discovered *the room was empty and shut up tightly from the inside!*

It became a regular occurrence for Jim Williams to call the police because he felt someone was in the house. He would have the policemen walk through and examine the residence; they never encountered anything.

One afternoon Jim opened the door and a captain was there to inform him that due to the numerous calls made to this address, the chief had decided to start sending a bill the next time they were called out on a false alarm. As the captain was explaining the chief's wishes, the organ started playing very loudly. Jim looked at the officer and said, "Captain, I am here alone and I don't own a player organ." Both men walked into the parlor and watched as the keys on the organ were being played on their own. That's when the police started taking Jim more seriously.

It got to be so bad that Jim had an Episcopal bishop from Atlanta come to Savannah and perform an exorcism on the house. Now, I tell people Jim must have made a large donation to get the bishop, but everyone liked Jim. Jim followed the bishop through the house as he sprinkled holy water and said the rites of exorcism. There was peace in the house for about two weeks, Jim said, and then the ghosts were back. Evidently they are not Episcopalian ghosts!

DAVENPORT HOUSE

Isaiah Davenport built his house in 1820, right after the second great fire. A master builder, he moved here from Rhode Island to help rebuild the city. Many structures in the historic district today were designed and built by Davenport.

This house was the first success story of the Historic Savannah Foundation. Slated for demolition in 1954 by the Goette Funeral Home next door—which needed the space for parking—the nucleus of what became the foundation, seven white-sneakered old belles, saved it. They borrowed the money from the C&S bank and bought the house, turning it into a museum and gift shop instead. Davenport House is still their biggest source of income today. Since then, the HSF has helped save and restore hundreds of buildings.

The front entrance, with the welcoming stairway and the heart shaped boot scrapers, is indicative of the dirt streets of a bygone era. Many people come to Savannah having read Eugenia Price's novels (this is her Mackay House) or have heard about the Historic Savannah Foundation and want to see the house. A creature with claws, fangs and a tail haunts this stairway. Many have seen this creature and have lived to tell the tale. Visitors walk up either side of the front stairs, thinking that to be the entrance. They go up to the front door and realize it is not. That is when they notice the cat. As they head downstairs, the cat rubs along their legs and purrs. Now, no one saw the cat going up and that's a wonder since the cat is so huge: a very large orange and white tabby cat. Visitors open the door of the gift shop on the Habersham Street side of the house, and the cat bolts inside. They begin to browse amongst the souvenirs and then they remember the cat. They inquire at the front desk about the *huge tabby*. The person working at the register will look at them oddly and reply, "What cat? There hasn't been a cat here since this became a museum in 1955."

Many people see the cat to this very day and I have had a number of guests on my tours comment about contact with the tabby cat. One man said he had visited the house earlier and had encountered the cat. He was standing at the top of the stairs on the second floor listening to the guide talk about the rooms. Excessive foot traffic causes wear and tear, so the upper rooms are cordoned off and visitors can only peer in from the top of the landing. The man distinctly felt a large cat purr as it rubbed against his leg. He looked down and saw nothing. He thought he had imagined the whole thing, until he heard my story.

The most recounted haunting has to do with the early days of the museum in the 1960's. At that time tourists had the full run of the house. There were no scheduled tours and the upper rooms were accessible; you could even visit the attic. The attic had a display of Victorian toys and lots of visitors enjoyed the toy exhibit. One day at closing, 4:55 in the afternoon, two ladies were leaving as the gift shop clerk went to lock up behind them. They turned and asked the clerk, "But what about the little girl in the attic?"

The clerk had kept up with everyone who came and went that day. The two ladies were the only visitors left in the museum. "What little girl?" she asked. "The little girl in the attic, playing with the toys," they replied.

The three ladies became very concerned. The clerk locked the door and went upstairs to find the girl. She came back down and said there was no one in the attic. All three searched the house and found no one.

The clerk looked out of the second floor window and saw a small girl dressed in a white dress with long golden curls. The other ladies were summoned. "That's the girl we saw in the attic."

Concerned for the girl's safety, the three ladies went into the garden. Again the clerk locked the door as they exited. The little girl was no longer in the garden, so they thought she might have gone to the front of the house. They walked into Columbia Square searching, but she was nowhere to be found. The ladies looked up at the house to see the girl gazing back at them from the top left dormer window.

I have been in the square with groups when someone will ask, "Who's the little girl in the top left window of that house?" and they have no idea that he or she is looking at a ghost.

KEHOE HOUSE

The Kehoe House is a fireproof structure and that's important in a town that burns on a regular basis. The entire structure is brick and all the ornamentation on the outside of the house is neither stone nor wood; it's cast iron. From the dormer windows on the roof to the columns and the entrance stairs, all of it is cast iron. Built by a man who owned an iron foundry, for the safety of his family, he could also show off his work to a potential client.

Mr. Kehoe died in 1908. His widow outlived him by many years, but legend has it that upon her death she requested that her family take her to the Catholic Cemetery located east of town in the most elaborate carriage they could find. The Kehoes didn't pay her any attention and when she died they put her coffin in the back of an old wooden cart and took it to the cemetery. *She jumped right back into the house and has been there ever since.* A lady in white haunts the hallways of the house. After the death of Mrs. Kehoe, her family moved two squares south to the streetcar suburbs of the Victorian District, and the house became a mortuary. For 65 years this was the Goette Funeral Home. The morgue, or embalming room, was located in the basement.

Along the President Street side of the house you'll notice a section of the granite border has been removed, and that's where they slid the coffins in and out of the basement. The bodies were put in the coffins and taken up the back stairs to the front parlor. Guests having breakfast in this B&B today are dining in what was once the Viewing Room. (I suggested a coffin covered with a smorgasbord, you know, Bloody Marys, cold cuts, and finger food...)

The mortuary closed in 1972, and a syndicate of men including Joe Namath and Terry Bradshaw purchased the Kehoe House intending to turn it into a gentlemen's club, much like the Playboy chain. Fortunately for us, bunnies never hopped around the house and it sat vacant for the next twenty years. That's when the present owner bought it and turned it into an historic inn, one of the finest in the South and definitely one of the most haunted.

I could spend hours telling of eyewitness accounts from this house, but the best one happened in the fall of 2004: I was standing with about twenty people in Columbia Square talking about the house when a man walked out of the beautiful leaded glass entry doors and said, "Robert, they told me inside I had to come out and tell you guys what happened last night."

He and his wife were staying on the second floor in the room on the front right above the parlor. They had been in the room for the past two nights, having a big time watching the ghost tour groups from their window. The second night the last tour came by and he and his wife went to bed. At 12:01 a.m., both were awakened by a bloodcurdling scream. A woman shrieked and someone fell down the stairs right outside their door.

They jumped out of the bed and ran out into the hallway. The couple in the adjoining room—Mrs. Kehoe's room—jumped out of their bed and ran out into the hall also. All four of them heard the woman scream and then fall, but they saw no one. He had no motivation to make up the story; it had happened just the night before.

There are lots of ghosts in this house. A family lived upstairs when this was a mortuary; they had the entire upper floor and many spoke of seeing a nurse. It seems this nurse has been seen by members of the Kehoe family, the undertakers, as well as people who stay at the inn today.

At the top of the beautiful mahogany staircase are four bedroom doors. The nurse seems to favor two particular doors. She's a very large woman with a peaked cap. Everyone comments how starched she is.

HAUNTINGS!

No one knows who she is or who her patients were, but as far as I can tell she's been on duty for almost eighty years and if she encounters you at the top of the stairs, *she will shush you.*

Shh!

LADY IN WHITE

My friend, Phyllis, worked as the night innkeeper at the Kehoe House for six years. She never heard or felt anything for the first four years working there and she never gave it a thought.

Then she saw the Lady in White. A lot of people have seen the Lady in White in the hallways and Phyllis saw her in the basement hallway.

Phyllis walked through the front entrance and felt a cold chill right down to her marrow. Later she was in the kitchen preparing a fruit plate for breakfast the next morning, working with her head down, when someone walked in the kitchen door. She looked up, but no one was there.

Later she was sitting at the front desk typing on her computer when someone came down the stairs directly in front of her. She looked up, but she saw nothing. She knew something was getting ready to happen.

August in Savannah is miserable. Ninety-eight degree heat with ninety-eight percent humidity. It's miserable if you aren't from here; it's miserable if you are from here. I've seen people literally melt. Some visitors take three showers a day. When Phyllis came to work that night everyone was out of towels. She had been in the basement three times in an hour gathering towels from the linen closet in the basement hallway. No problem. The fourth time, as she walked down the mahogany staircase, she stepped on the last step and the hair on her neck stood straight up. She got what my daddy used to call 'chicken skin': she had goose bumps all over.

Phyllis stepped into the hallway and there stood the Lady in White. She was hovering at the end of the hallway about a foot off the ground. Phyllis said it was like someone had knocked the wind out of her. She couldn't breathe. She said all she could do was stand there. The apparition mesmerized her. She was frozen as if her feet were glued to the floor. After a short period of time she started to rock back and forth, just standing there swaying. (She thinks her body was trying to calm her.) But her eyes were still fixed on the ghost.

Phyllis told me that she finally ripped her eyes away then looked at her feet. She prayed to God, "Lord, please make her go away." She looked up and the apparition was gone. Phyllis ran up the stairs and collapsed in the chair behind the desk. She sat there and hyperventilated for many minutes.

I spoke to Joe, who worked with Phyllis, about two weeks after the incident. He told me he found her like that. "Clammy, breathing hard, visibly shaken, I knew she was frightened." He poured her a cup of coffee, put some cognac in it, and after her second cup she began breathing properly.

MRS. KEHOE'S ROOM

I have two eyewitness accounts from this room. The first Phyllis said; happened in October 2004. The second occurred in December to a couple staying in the room.

The room was occupied on Octoberfest weekend. The first Saturday in October a barge is set in the Savannah River, with Disney World quality fireworks starting at nine in the evening. Most residents and visitors go to Bay Street or River Street and watch the fireworks from there. That weekend everyone had gone except the lady staying in Mrs. Kehoe's room. Her husband went but she didn't feel well. The innkeeper was downstairs. They were the only two people in the inn. Nine o'clock, the guest was lying in bed when the fireworks began and it was loud. The boom of the fireworks shook the windows and rattled the doors.

The guest was lying there listening to the tattoo of the fireworks—boom, boom! When she heard a loud rap at the door, she approached and saw the knob turning as if someone were trying to open it. She asked who was there. A young girl's voice said, "We're scared. Can we come in? We're scared."

The guest replied in a loud voice, "Where are your parents?" The child's voice replied, "We don't know where they are, we're scared." In a very stern voice, like any other parent, the guest replied, "It's just fireworks, go back to bed." She heard nothing further and went back to bed.

The next morning the guest went downstairs and asked Phyllis which room the children were in, as she wanted to speak to their parents. Quite perplexed, the innkeeper explained that the inn hadn't had any children for at least three weeks.

Now that was in October. Two months later in December, a couple from Ohio was in the same room and I spoke to both of them about their experience. The husband told me his wife had planned the whole day for them. They had spent the morning shopping, then went to Mrs. Wilkes' for lunch, and went shopping some more. About four-thirty in the afternoon they returned to their room.

They dropped their purchases on the floor, and the wife lay down for a nap. She said she was dead tired and it didn't take her seconds to fall asleep. As soon as she dozed off someone sat on the edge of her bed. She opened her eyes and saw a small girl with long blond hair. She immediately thought it was her daughter, but then she remembered their daughter was in Ohio with relatives.

Her husband walked into the room and saw the little girl. The girl smiled at both of them and slowly vanished. The wife got up and together she and her husband went to the foot of the bed and both could see the impression in the bedclothes where the little girl had been sitting.

GHOSTLY, FRIENDLY EXPERIENCE

The Kehoe House has a guest register on a console on the left as you walk in. Guests are encouraged to sign the book and leave comments. Phyllis used to go through it now and again and put red dots next to the entries that had to do with any paranormal encounters.

I went through the book one afternoon and found many entries, one of which I took the time to copy verbatim. There were two ladies; I didn't write their names, just what they said: "What a beautiful city," it began, "and what a wonderful inn. Stay in room 301 if you want a *ghostly, friendly experience.*"

I asked Phyllis about room 301 and she took me upstairs and showed it to me. Room 301 is located on the top floor in the back of the house, on the State Street side. It's a corner room with a rather pleasant view. There are two single beds, so it's usually the last room to be rented. Most people who stay in the room experience the same phenomena:

They are sitting on the bed or reclining in one of the wing chairs, reading or watching the television, when someone or something will stroke the back of their hand and sometimes lift them by the elbows as if to pick them up and kiss them on the cheek; *a ghostly, friendly experience.*

I have often wondered if it is a cold kiss or a warm kiss? Either way it's too friendly for me.

I have been conducting walking tours since the fall of 1997, and have to admit that I've rarely encountered anything of a paranormal nature. One occasion was in the fall of 2003, and I had a fairly large group on the 9 p.m. tour, about twenty people. Since mine is a family tour and fun for all ages there were about four small children that night, ranging from toddlers to adolescents.

We had an exceptionally nice night and they were a good audience and seemed to be really interested in the walk. Half way through the tour I was standing at the foot of the front stairs of the Kehoe House, telling the story of Phyllis and the Lady in White. The children were lined up in front of the adults and were rapt with attention.

As I was talking, I noticed the children were all staring at the balcony on the third floor above Mrs. Kehoe's room. I turned, looked and saw nothing so I continued to give my narrative. They were so intent on that particular spot that I glanced up there again and saw nothing. I stopped and asked them what was so interesting because their behavior had piqued my interest.

"You don't see the little girl?" said one child, and with that the whole group looked up but there was no little girl. I said, "What little girl?" And the child said, "The little girl on the balcony." I looked again and sure enough there was a small child standing at the rail of the balcony. She was just tall enough that we could see her head above the handrail and she had long blonde hair. I turned back to the group so that they would acknowledge having seen the girl and they all just looked at me as if nothing out of the ordinary had occurred.

I looked again and she was gone. I stopped speaking and walked around the south side of the house and saw no one; the balcony was dark and no movement could be seen. I came back to the group and asked if anyone else had seen the child with only the children responding in the affirmative. It gave me quite a stir but I continued with my tour.

The next day I called and asked the innkeeper if they had any children staying in the inn and if so were they in the room on the third floor. The innkeeper responded that there were no children in the Kehoe House that she was aware of. I will never forget that little girl. She was looking down from the balcony right at our group. I noticed her for a few seconds but none of the other adults in the group saw anyone. The only ones to see her were the children on the tour...and me!

ANNA

The 17Hundred90 is the oldest operating inn in Savannah and has one of the best restaurants in the city. Sitting in the dining room enjoying a wonderful meal, diners notice some of the beams are charred and burnt. The structure has burned to the brick foundations twice in the great fires of the city, and salvageable beams were saved.

There are fourteen romantic rooms upstairs and all of the rooms are the same: four-poster beds, reproduction period furniture and exposed brick fireplaces. A favorite with honeymooners, the 17Hundred90 offers a great breakfast in the courtyard of their sister property, the President's Quarters, right across Lincoln Street.

Only room 204 is different; it has a resident poltergeist. You can stay in room 204 any night of the week. But when you make your reservation or check in, the management will tell you room 204 is haunted because they don't want you to ask for your money back.

One of the most written about and documented ghosts in the Deep South inhabits room 204; her name is Anna and she's a poltergeist. Poltergeist means "noisy spirit" in German and we interpret it as noisy ghost. It also is usually associated with the tragic death of a young woman. That's what we have here, a tragic death and a noisy ghost.

The original townhouse at 225 East President Street dates to the 1790's. Built by Steele White, a merchant in the colony, he was a successful importer-exporter and very wealthy man. In his early sixties he imported a child bride from Ireland and ensconced her in room 204 until the wedding.

The wedding never took place, for within days of her arrival Anna threw herself from the roof, broke her neck and died in room 204 twelve hours later. Anna still inhabits this room, and she's seen quite often in other parts of the inn as well. Guests and employees of the inn see Anna on the stairs and in the hallways. She will stare at couples as they pass. Many people hear a woman crying in the wee hours—she's a poltergeist, a noisy ghost.

Guests using the front stairs will find Anna's visage sitting and crying in the early hours before dawn. People out late will notice a woman sitting and weeping on the stoop, and when they approach to give comfort, she disappears right before their eyes.

I frequently speak to guests who stay in room 204—Business people and single people sleep through the night and don't have a bit of trouble. Couples have trouble in that room. Lying in bed at night they are awakened by the sound of the chest of drawers slamming against the wall, *Crash!* Or they're asleep and the whole bed rises off the floor and settles down, *Crash!* Why they are still in the room after that, I have no idea!

Anna loves to play with the fixtures. The lights go on and off all hours of the day and night. She loves to play with the water. The innkeeper, housekeepers and guests will tell you that the shower comes on all by itself. The toilet flushes at two or three in the morning and flushes incessantly. Anna loves to play with the toilet.

There's a telephone in room 204 that rings in and of itself. Those answering the phone hear a woman sobbing on the other end of the line. If that bothers you—and it bothers most people—unplug the phone *and it still rings.* There is a report of the phone driving one guest crazy, so he yanked the phone out of the wall and it started ringing in his hand. That's when I would drop the phone, go downstairs, and ask for another room!

Anna's biggest prank is my favorite prank: she steals ladies' lingerie. Ladies lay out something for the next day, turn around, and it's gone. There has never been a cache of lingerie found in the inn, as it just disappears.

I have many eyewitness accounts from this establishment over the years and every one of them concerns couples, but whenever anything happens, it usually occurs when the lady is out of the room. People who work there tell me it only happens to couples that are in love, because Anna knows the difference. There may be something to that because every occurrence that I have heard about happened when the man was in the room by himself.

I had a couple on the tour one night relate to the group what had transpired when they were in the room the night before. They had just checked in and unpacked. He was surfing the TV looking for something to watch while his wife was downstairs gathering brochures from the lobby. He said the whole time she was gone the TV started acting up and the remote wouldn't work but that as soon as she walked in the TV went back to normal and the remote started operating properly.

She went into the bathroom and while she was in there the TV picture started rolling, going from black to gray and not responding whatsoever to the remote. As soon as she stepped back into the room the TV went back to normal and everything was fine.

One of the best eyewitness accounts occurred to the manager and maitre d' while they were having dinner in June 2004. A newly wedded couple checked in late, and was given room 204.

The maitre d' routinely stops answering the telephone after 9:30 at night because the kitchen closes at ten o'clock and there is no point in answering. He said the phone started to ring and he ignored it, but continued to ring for five minutes. So finally he picked the phone up and it was the bride in room 204. She was very upset and seemed quite shaken.

The maitre d' asked what was the matter and she said, "My husband is on the floor. He won't get up. Please help me!" and she hung up. The maitre d' and the manager proceeded upstairs, finding the bride at the door waiting for them. They asked her what happened. The bride said they got in the room, unpacked the suitcases, and undressed. He went to bed. She went in the bathroom. When she came out of the bathroom, he was on the floor and he wouldn't get up so she called for assistance.

The two men went into room 204 and found the groom in his underwear under the four-poster bed very shaken. It took them quite awhile to coax him out from under the bed. They sat him down on the bed and gave him some water to drink. He became coherent and they asked him what had happened.

He said the same thing as his wife. They got in the room and unpacked. He and his wife undressed and she went into the bathroom. He went to bed. He's lying there waiting for his bride and he dozed off. As soon as he fell asleep, he felt someone sit on the bed next to him.

The bride was a blond, but when the groom opened his eyes he saw a woman with shiny black hair sitting next to him. She had on a long white nightgown. He said she smiled at him. He rolled away from her off the other side, went under the bed, and he wasn't coming out.

The manager moved the couple into room 205. The groom was still in his underwear. He didn't wait to get dressed. He just wanted another room.

RICHARDSON-OWENS-THOMAS HOUSE

One of the finest house museums in the South, definitely the finest in Savannah, is the Richardson-Owens-Thomas house which stands on Oglethorpe Square at Abercorn and President Streets. It has been a house museum since 1950.

Three generations of the same family lived here and everything on display is original to the house.

I highly recommend this museum. It is open seven days a week and admission only costs eight dollars to enter. You will be very surprised at just how modern this house is. Built in 1818 for Richard Richardson by William Jay, a twenty-year-old architect from Bath, England, this Regency style structure features iron supports, a slate roof, and twenty-three inch thick walls. It's also fireproof.

This house has been featured in five different books about hauntings. There are several stories associated with this home and all seem to indicate that its old inhabitants are still here. The last owner of the house was Margaret Thomas. She died in 1949, and left this house to the Telfair Museum of Art, which operates it as an interpretive history exhibit.

Margaret's bedroom faces the iron veranda located on the President Street side of the home. She was born in that bedroom in 1860 and died eighty-nine years later in the same bed. That bed is still in the room and Margaret still abides there. She's still in the house, along with a few of her ancestors.

Margaret is seen quite often in this house. She is seen in the front parlor but more often than not she is seen in the garden after dark. It's not unusual to see a lady walking in her garden after dark but this is a museum: no one lives here. People who live in the townhouses on State Street or stay in the President's Quarters nearby see a lady walking around the garden at night.

We are not going to discuss Margaret. However, we are going to talk about Jim Williams. He is the central character in the book *Midnight in the Garden of Good and Evil,* and the only person in the United States to be tried for the same murder four times. He was acquitted on his last trial. He had a lot of money, and he finally found a good lawyer.

If Jim hadn't become notorious for his infamous trials, he would have been famous for his preservation efforts. I tell people that before the Savannah College of Art and Design arrived in Savannah, Jim set the bar for quality in the local restoration movement. He restored over fifty homes in the Historic District and it would take me hours to walk you around and show you. He didn't have anything to do with restoring the Owens-Thomas House; he was just visiting.

Margaret Thomas spent half of her life in this house an old maid. She rented out the entire upper floor, the carriage house, and slave quarters as apartments and well into the 1980's the Telfair did the same thing for income. Jim had a friend who occupied the entire upper floor as his apartments. Nice digs. This was in the early Sixties and Jim and his business partner were visiting.

Jim and his partner were sitting in the front room on the top floor overlooking the square. He said they had been there for about an hour talking antiques. There were only three men in the room when Jim and his partner noticed two very odd things: The first thing they noticed was that a man materialized in the back of the room. He just came out of nowhere. Jim said three men were in the room and all of a sudden there was a fourth party.

The other odd thing the two men noticed was that their host didn't see anything. He just sat there talking. Jim described the ghost in detail: he was an equestrian of the nineteenth century, wearing tall black riding boots, jodhpur slacks, a swallow-tail jacket, and carrying a riding crop in his hand. Jim nicknamed him 'The Horseman'. Jim had a sense of humor when it came to ghosts.

Jim was intently watching the apparition move back and forth across the room when abruptly the ghost stopped, turned and walked right through the two-seater couch their host was sitting on. The host just sat there and kept talking. The ghost came and hovered over Jim. The ghost seemed to be interested in him.

That's when Jim noticed two funny things: the ghost had blue eyes, and not only that, but he noticed the specter's forehead and there was sweat on his brow. *Only in Savannah is it hot enough to make a ghost sweat.* He looked like he had come in from a hard ride. The whole time he was standing over Jim he was like the Cheshire Cat. Then he slowly vanished and the last thing they saw of the apparition was his lingering smile as he disappeared from sight.

MARINE HOSPITAL

The U.S. Public Health Service building at Drayton and York Streets was constructed in 1905 and was an active hospital until the 1980's, when the Public Health Service was shut down. It became a day clinic and was used as such until 2003, when the clinic moved to East Broad Street into new quarters. Purchased recently by SCAD, it will be converted into administrative offices.

It's huge, almost 70,000 square feet, and it sits on Oglethorpe Square. There are bound to be encounters. The building is probably the most haunted structure in town.

Many people on my tour have taken photos of the hospital at night and they are covered with orbs. The first time I saw one of these pictures, back in 1997, I said, "Yeah, someone blew soap bubbles and took a flash photo!" That's what orbs look like, bubbles. They are not bubbles, they're orbs. One theory states that an orb is energy being transferred from a source (street lights or radio signals, cell phones etc.) to a ghost so they can manifest themselves to us. According to physics, energy being transferred takes the shape of a sphere. This may not be a conscious thing on the part of the ghost, just a natural way for them to gain energy in order to manifest.

I have seen many photos of orbs since then, and, depending on who may be in the group, this building is covered with them. There seems to be a direct connection between some perceptive people and the hauntings. Some people interest ghosts. I know that from the walking tours; certain people draw apparitions out.

The top floor of this hospital was the quarantine ward and for its first fifty years, when a sailor came into this port with a fever, he was put up there. This was before the cause of these fevers was known, before we had antibiotics or penicillin. In order to quarantine the victim from the local population, he was put up there. If he made it to the ward, he had been lucky to make it into the port past the "lazaretto". Every port has one. It is an Italian term for a building used as a Pest House or quarantine station. Usually located off shore or inland before the port's harbor, it is an anchorage area used for quarantine.

The Works Progress Administration (WPA) Guidebook for Georgia describes this hospital as the quarantine station for the port. Sick passengers and sailors were kept there. Any ship with fever would be told to anchor at the lazaretto and anyone with fever would be taken off and put in the pest house. The ship would then be allowed to come into the harbor. Savannah even has a Lazaretto Creek, the last bridge on the way to Tybee Island at the mouth of the Savannah River. When you cross the bridge today, the north side is the area where the Pest House was located and to the south the cemetery where victims of the fevers were buried.

So if a sailor made it into this port with a fever, he was put into the quarantine ward. If he didn't have a deadly fever going in, he did after being put up there. Ninety percent of the patients died there. We're not talking dozens. We're talking tens of dozens of men died there. It is one of the most haunted spots in the South. Take a photograph and the hospital is covered with orbs. I have a photo that a lady e-mailed me. She took the walking tour on December 2, 2004, and snapped a picture from the corner of Drayton and President Streets. It looks like fireworks! The building is covered with orbs!

I have been walking ghost tours by this building each night since 1997. Three years ago, I was walking with a group on President Street, telling the story of Alice Riley, when a couple walked up and asked the group if we had seen any ghosts. We all chuckled and said no. They said, "Look at this," and pulled out their camera. I knew the couple as members of the Searchers, a group of residents who study the paranormal. The group interviews people who have experienced spectral activity and spend the night in haunted houses. They have electro-magnetic sensors, temperature gauges and digital cameras. They search for hauntings. It was the 9 p.m. tour; they were out for a walk with their digital camera looking for paranormal activity. Both walked by the hospital and noticed the front door open. So they ran in and took a picture of the empty staircase, waited for the little red light to quit blinking and then took another. They left as quickly as they had come. They switched on the digital camera and an image came up. It was a darkened stairway, illuminated by a flash. But the stairs weren't empty. There were three distinct orbs on the stairs. He switched to the next image; it was the same darkened stairway illuminated by a flash. Only this time there weren't three of them. The whole stairway was full of them. Each stair tread had at least one or two orbs. From top to bottom, it was covered with them. So now I tell people not only is that one of the most haunted upper floors in the city, but now they are starting to come downstairs!

COLONIAL PARK CEMETERY

Colonial Park Cemetery was the second burial ground for the city. From 1750 to 1850, a hundred years of Savannah citizenry was buried there and for the life of this cemetery it was called the Old Brick Burial or Brick Wall Cemetery. There was a two-foot wide, seven-foot tall brick wall that ran all the way around it.

The Old Brick Cemetery has many illustrious burials. Here lie the early colonists, the patriots of '76, heroes of the Mexican War, merchants and civilians who by public spirit and zealous enterprise built Savannah.

The original cemetery was set aside in 1733 at Bull and York Streets from Whitaker to South Broad, as laid out by General Oglethorpe. It filled fast with yellow fever victims. After seventeen years the city needed a new cemetery, so they purchased the Christ Church burial plot and that became the city's cemetery. A portion of the original wall remains on the east side and it is covered with tombstones that were knocked over by Federal troops bivouacked there while General Sherman occupied the town toward the end of the Civil War. The wall stood almost fifty years after the cemetery was closed to burials.

The cemetery was closed because it was full. It doesn't look full now. There are less than 600 markers in this cemetery but it is full with over 8,000 documented burials, and in the south end of the six-acre graveyard—under the tennis courts and playground—are mass burials from three yellow fever epidemics. What are missing are the tombstones. The cemetery used to be packed with them. The Chicora Foundation of Columbia, SC, did a high tech survey on the burial ground and found graves everywhere. They used the little flags like the telephone company uses and the cemetery looked like a pincushion. The Union Army used the walled cemetery to quarter horses and assemble wagons so they removed the tombstones. Many of the existing stones were refitted in recent efforts to reconstitute the burial ground.

There are reports of how the Union Army did horrendous damage. The Yankees pulled the bodies from the crypts, stole the gold teeth and the jewelry, and burned the coffins for firewood. One account tells of how a Sergeant rigged up a pot bellied stove in a family vault and slept with the deceased. Many of the stones were moved and some stones were defaced. The soldiers also played pranks. The troops occupied the burial ground for ten weeks and after the first few days they were bored to tears so they changed the dates on many of the stones, the proof of which remains today. One is a table ledger grave belonging to the Long family: two brothers and their wives, to the right as you enter the main gate. It's quite legible:

Henry Long is 128, Michael Long is 132, Elizabeth is 143, and Mary is 168. They didn't have great longevity in the Long family, the Yankees put a "1" in front of each age with their bayonets, and they changed the ages.

When the occupation ended, the wooden gates were nailed shut and the Old Brick Cemetery sat idle and in disrepair for many years. The wall was removed in 1896 and the burial ground became an open promenade. The perimeter wall was removed on three sides and on the Abercorn Street side they added a sidewalk. The markers were moved, but the graves are still there. Not long ago, the Laurel Grove Cemetery found a large stack of stones. After checking the burial roles, they were able to determine that the stones came from the Old Brick Cemetery. The stones were moved but not the remains.

In 1913 the Daughters of the American Revolution installed the gate at Oglethorpe and Abercorn. At that time there was a family vault where the DAR wanted a gate so they removed the top of the vault. The family is still there under the entrance with no marker. Merely by entering the cemetery through the main gate you are walking on the dead.

DUELING

"Set honor in one eye,
And death in the other,
And I will look on both indifferently,
For, let the gods so speed me as I love,
The name of honor more than I fear death."
                              Charles Colquitt Jones

"Dueling seems almost as remote from today
as the feudal age out of which it sprang. It was
a last, long-lingering remnant of the customs
of chivalry and found its grave in the new con-
ditions of life that came after the south's war
of separate nationality."
                              Joel Chandler Harris

"A man has a right to defend his honor..."
                              James Edward Oglethorpe

The Brick Wall Cemetery was one of the favorite dueling grounds for the gentlemen of the city. No one knew what they were doing until the shots were fired. The brick wall concealed their actions until it was too late. So the city fathers removed the wall and the burial ground became an open promenade that gave no cover. Prohibited from fighting duels there, matters of honor were moved to the east end of River Street at Fort Wayne—the same man Fort Wayne, Indiana, is named after, 'Mad' Anthony Wayne, a famous Revolutionary War hero.

When duels were broken up by societies intent on eradicating the practice, parties took small boats across the Savannah River in the wee hours of the morning and fought their matters of honor on the old dusty road to Charleston, so no one could molest them. They didn't like anyone to fool with them when they were trying to kill each other; it was 'bad form'.

The first recorded duel was between two of Oglethorpe's officers; one killed the other with a sword. The founder of the colony didn't do anything about it because it was a matter of honor, a matter amongst gentlemen, and that's the way Southern society felt about dueling right up to the twentieth century.

The most famous duel to be fought in Colonial Cemetery is located where the temple form monument is, the most illuminated memorial at night. That is where Button Gwinnett is buried, one of the three signers of the Declaration of Independence from the State of Georgia, and he was killed less than a year after signing. (Gwinnett County is named for him.) May 1777, he fought a duel with Lachlan McIntosh. (McIntosh County is named for him.) They fought with pistols at three paces; that's about nine to ten feet. McIntosh's second was Major Habersham, the man who built the Pink House on Reynolds Square. The Major asked him, "Are we going to start you back to back and walk three paces?" (Which would have been six paces or eighteen feet).

McIntosh responded, "Oh no, you will mark off three paces. We will face each other and see what we're about."

Two men with pistols at ten feet, but apparently they didn't mean to kill each other because each shot the other in the right leg. Unfortunately for Button Gwinnett his leg shattered, his artery burst and he bled to death. Doctors couldn't deal with arterial wounds back then; he died two days later. He is buried somewhere near his monument. Just like Aaron Burr, Lachian McIntosh was tried for murder; everyone knew it was a duel though, so he was acquitted. He left town in disgrace, having killed one of the signers of the Declaration of Independence. No one cared for McIntosh anymore. He moved north and spent the winter with Washington at Valley Forge.

McIntosh became a war hero and rose to the rank of general, and returned in full honor and lived in Savannah the rest of his life! He is buried in the same cemetery with Gwinnett, on the Abercorn Street side.

Just like Burr—who had to answer whenever someone brought up Alexander Hamilton—anytime anyone brought up Button Gwinnett, McIntosh would answer, "The reason Gwinnett died was because he had a poor physician."

Of course, *it was the doctor's fault;* it didn't have anything to do with the fact McIntosh blew his leg off.

CITY HOTEL

The Gwinnett-McIntosh duel was fought at three paces with pistols; that's close range. In the antebellum or pre-Civil War era, it was commonplace for men to fight at such close quarters. Behind establishments like the City Hotel or the Marshall House men would fight a handkerchief duel.

In the lane behind the Marshall House was a carriage turnaround; today it is the atrium for the 45 Bistro. Carriages would enter the lane, passengers would be let out at the back of the inn and the horse and conveyance would turn and leave. Many duels were fought in these areas, duels of quick action, not the formal kind; matters of honor that had to be settled on the spot between planters, merchants, ship captains, gamblers and pirates. There was no waiting period and hardly ever any seconds or witnesses. A handkerchief duel was fought in the heat of the moment between passionate and usually intoxicated combatants. One of them was probably a gentleman or some semblance thereof and he would have a handkerchief. You know how large a man's kerchief is, about ten to twelve inches across. The combatants grabbed a corner and stretched the cloth between them. Each would have his pistol held in their other hand by his side ready to fire. On the count of three, each would quickly raise his firearm to the other's head and fire. Usually one of the two would fall to his knees and say he was sorry or someone would have his head blown off.

THE SIX-PENCE PUB

The Six Pence Pub on Bull Street near Chippewa Square is a favorite with locals and tourists alike. A large contingent of expatriate Brits hang out on Tuesday nights. Outdoor seating, and the pub doesn't frown on well-behaved dogs when accompanied by their owners. There is an array of flags out front representing each member of Great Britain. An Irish flag proves there's no ill will and on St. Patrick's Day this place is packed and I mean *packed.*

The building itself dates to the 1910's, built on an antebellum foundation with two basements. It is very unusual to have a subterranean basement in the Historic District; most of the buildings in the district have elevated basements. To have two basements, one above the other, is unique.

There are a number of specters haunting this watering hole and over the years there have been numerous occurrences involving the paranormal. One of the past owners, Wendy, related how she came in one night, went through the kitchen and down the stairs to her office in the basement. When she approached the door, she got a queer feeling and a cold chill ran right through her.

She opened the door and the executive chair at the desk turned toward her and leaned forward and snapped back. It was as if someone had stood up out of the chair. Wendy said she felt a blast of cold air pass beside her as she stood in the open doorway. It took her a few moments to calm herself down. She took a deep breath, ran upstairs and out of the restaurant to her car and didn't return for two days.

Bonnie, the manager for years, would ignore me or feign indifference when I would inquire about paranormal activity. She would always say it was all nonsense and she didn't believe a word of it. One afternoon I was having lunch at the bar, speaking to a couple visiting our beautiful city and when they found out I was a tour-guide, naturally we started talking about hauntings. Bonnie leaned over the bar and asked, "Would you like to hear what happened to me?"

"By all means," I encouraged her.

She began, "It was late. The bartender wanted to leave early and he needed to give the waitress a ride home, so I told them to go on and I would clean up. I cleaned the dining room and the bar, then went downstairs and checked the thermostats on the walk-in coolers, turned off the lights, and returned upstairs. I set the air conditioner on 72 degrees and set the alarm by the front door, locked the door and went home. It was about 2:30 in the morning.

"The next morning, I got a call from the day manager and she was frantic. She asked me what had happened the night before and could I please come to the pub right away. Wondering what could possibly be so upsetting, I raced to the restaurant and found the staff standing out front.

"The windows were completely frosted over with moisture. The alarm was still set when we unlocked the door and walked inside. It was as cold as a freezer;

we went in and found the thermostat set on 60 degrees. We went downstairs to find every cooler warm and the thermostats set at 80°F. To top it all off, every bulb downstairs had been removed from the fixtures on the ceiling and neatly stacked on the floor below. "

A few years back, I was speaking to one of the bartenders and he related an incident that happened one night after hours. The staff had finished cleaning the dining room and were sitting at the bar having their first drink of the evening. The conversation turned to hauntings. There were personal stories shared and giggles all around as each told of their own experiences at the pub. A lull in the conversation caused them to think about the time of night and the location.

There was a distant sound of a gumball machine as the handle turns, the ball falls and hits the little door. The gumball machine was at that time located just to the left of the front door as you exit the bar. No one was by the door; it was locked, and there was no one else in the place.

Each started to laugh and dared the others to go look. So the bartender walked around the bar and lifted the little hatch and nothing came out! They all laughed and put the entire episode down to strong imaginings on their part. It didn't take minutes for them to finish their drinks and head for the door.

The waitress and busboy waited as the bartender set the alarm and exited the pub. He locked the deadbolt and lifted the mail slot to drop the cooler keys through for the next day's help, and as he lifted the mail slot, *a gumball rolled out!*

Another common occurrence the kitchen staff relates has to do with the dishes and the pots and pans. They seem to come alive. Many times the saucers or plates will stand on end and spin on their own. I have been in the bar when a cook will come out and say that a saucer in the middle of the stack just dislodged itself from the rest and sailed across the kitchen.

OH! SO MUCH BLOOD!

The last great fire in 1889 spared Chippewa Square. A whim of nature, the wind held the fire off the square and blew the flames east, destroying over half the city in 48 hours of terror. Three sides of this charming square are pre-Civil War or antebellum. Everything on the north side was destroyed; the rest of the square was saved. Most of the buildings date from the 1820's and 1830's, with a few built of wood, which is a rarity in a town with a history of fires.

One of the wooden structures at the corner of Bull and Perry Streets dates from the 1830's and is a beautiful Carpenter style house. There are a number of stories associated with this house and they all revolve around a young woman who is heard to scream, "Oh! So much blood!"

A gentleman and his family moved into the house in the 1870's and everything that happened to them is recorded in the newspapers of the day. The man was from Philadelphia and had come down to take a job with a local insurance company. The family arrived by steamboat to the wharves on River Street, and had a local moving company bring their furniture and belongings up the bluff and into the house.

It was near dusk when the last of the crates and furniture was loaded into the basement and on the parlor level. The gentleman told the movers because of the lateness of the hour to come back the next day and move their belongings upstairs. The family would have dinner on their crates and covered furniture.

The movers retired for the night and the family sat with a picnic on the parlor floor. They were eating when footsteps could be heard running from room to room upstairs and—as they wondered who could possibly be there—they heard a woman's voice screaming, "Oh! So much blood! Oh! So much blood!" The family ran upstairs and searched the entire upper floor and found no one there.

Then they heard the voice coming from below on the parlor level where they had been eating and ran downstairs to investigate. There was no one in sight. Thinking whoever it was could have gone out into the garden, the family ran outside to search the grounds, only to hear the woman screaming from inside. They spent the night at the Pulaski House Hotel and had the movers remove all their belongings the next morning.

One of the last owners of the house died recently; she was in her mid-nineties. She used to talk about the shades in the house. She wasn't talking about the window dressings; she was talking about ghosts. That's what the old gentry called ghosts, shades. She would say, "Oh, those shades, they kept me up all night, running from room to room and that poor woman, I wish she would just move on!"

That's the way most people in Savannah are with their ghosts: they just put up with them or tolerate them as if they were family, so to speak.

FOLEY HOUSE INN

Built in the 1890's after the last great conflagration, the Foley House is one of the most luxurious inns in the Historic District. In 1992, its owners wanted to open up the basement to the garden, so a large arch was installed in the basement wall to open into the courtyard. When workmen broke through the 18-inch thick brick wall, they found the petrified remains of a small-framed adult male. The only people that were here long enough to be petrified were natives.

The Native-Americans who lived on this bit of high ground when Oglethorpe and the colonists arrived were members of the Creek-Choctaw nation and called themselves Guale. Like the Choctaw, the Guale buried above ground in mounds, the higher up the social strata, the higher up the mound one was buried. Some of these mounds still exist in Georgia at Etowah and Coweta, as well as Ocmulgee and Muscogee, Alabama, and in the plains states. Many of these mounds and shell-middens left by the natives were destroyed by the colonists and used to fill low spots; the bits of bone, cloth and pottery didn't seem to bother anyone. As late as the 1950's, a large mound on Montgomery Crossroads—an old colonial road about 6 miles south of the Historic District—was destroyed as a public nuisance. It was bulldozed and the Board of Education built a middle school on top of the spoils. In the 1930's, the Corps of Engineers took out two of the largest Indian burial mounds on the east coast, the

Irene mounds. They did extensive archaeology on the site. We learned the seven ages of the mounds and a few artifacts were recovered. The mounds were leveled and the spoil was used to fill hundreds of acres of marshland to build the State Docks upriver at Port Wentworth.

When the builders were excavating the foundation of Foley House they found the petrified remains of a Guale local. The societal norm at that time would have been to discard it; that is what most people did when they found Indian remains. But evidently the builder didn't feel that way: to show a reverence for the grave, he bricked up the body in the building; one of the most bizarre mortar in-fill I've ever come across.

In the foyer of Foley House is a small cubbyhole used as a front desk and on the wall above it is a framed account from the local newspaper relating these facts. Part of the remains are in a drawer in an Anthropology lab at the University of Georgia in Athens. I think it's a shame, though; they ought to re-inter the poor old Indian in the earth where he was found.

JULIETTE GORDON LOW BIRTHPLACE

The most documented haunting in Savannah is the Juliette Gordon Low birthplace. Eyewitness accounts, police reports, and Gordon family diaries all attest to this fact. Juliette was born here Halloween night 1860. She told people all her life that she was born on All Hallow's Eve, the night of witches and goblins.

Juliette founded the Girl Scouts in America in the house in 1912, and since 1953 the house has been run by a big concern on Fifth Avenue, New York: the Girl Scouts of the USA. If you work there as a house guide or docent you are not allowed to talk about ghosts so as not to scare the little scouts or offend religious sensibilities. I go in there all the time and pick on them but the ladies won't tell me anything.

The History Channel came through there in the late 1990's and did a series entitled *Haunted Cities, Haunted Savannah.* They re-enacted the haunting at the Low birthplace among others. The house is open to the public six days a week and I highly recommend it.

William Washington Gordon purchased the house in 1822 from U.S. Senator James Moore Wayne, the first Georgian to sit on the U.S. Supreme Court, and since then it has been in the Gordon family. The Girl Scouts are an extension of Juliette's family, still the same owners so to speak.

William Washington Gordon II was born in this house and it is here that he brought his wife Nellie Kinzie to live in 1858. They had a long love affair and both lived into the twentieth century. Willie died in 1912, the same year Juliette started the Girl Scouts; Nellie died five years later.

The Kinzies were a founding family of Chicago and daughter Eleanor, "Nellie," was renowned as the first child baptized in the city. Her father, uncle, and two brothers were all Union officers. She remained loyal to her husband, however, and stayed in the house in Savannah until the end. The end being when General Sherman occupied or liberated the city, however you wish to look at it.

Willie was the first Confederate officer to become a general in the U.S. Army. He served in both the Civil

War and the Spanish-American War. For a strong lady like Nellie Gordon, she completely fell apart when her husband died. From all the accounts I've read and heard, she was prostrate at his feet on his deathbed. She had a nervous breakdown.

She told her family, "I can't live without him. If Willie goes, I will have to go too." Willie told her twice emphatically that when she died he would come back to get her, and with the second promise he passed away. She, however, returned to full mental health and lived with a sound mind the rest of her life. She told her family the last five years of her life not to mourn for her when she died because Willie was coming back to get her.

And Willie did come back. In the throes of Nellie's last illness, at age 82, bed-ridden for the last six months and emaciated, the doctor said she would expire at any moment. Her five adult children were at her side, Juliette among them, waiting for Nellie to die. In the adjoining bedroom, the general's old bedroom, was Margaret. As a daughter-in-law, she wasn't part of the immediate family. She had already said good-bye to her mother-in-law and she was reading to pass the time. Trying to keep from being overcome with grief, the reading gave her something to do.

The History Channel had Margaret's son, Arthur Gordon, on the show. He recounted what he had grown up hearing and recited what was written in his mother's diary from that period. Arthur Gordon was an accomplished, published writer who passed away recently in his mid eighties. He was past editor in chief of Guidepost Magazine and a sincere man.

Margaret had been in the room reading for quite awhile when all of a sudden the door to the hallway opened and Willie walked in. She said he had on his favorite gray suit, had his hat in his hand and had a look of gladness on his face. He signaled with his hand to be silent and as he approached his wife's bedroom door, it opened and closed 'in and of itself' as Willie passed through. Margaret was sitting there with the book in her lap, aghast!

Moments later the bedroom door opened and Margaret's husband walked in to tell her that his mother had died and the strangest thing happened just before she passed. All five children wrote something similar in their diaries Juliette wrote that from a mask of death, her mother sat bolt right up and took on the countenance of a young bride. One of her brothers wrote that she sat bolt right up and looked like a bride looking for her bride's maids, then fell over dead.

What Margaret's husband told her fit in with what she had seen, so she told him that she had seen Willie, but her husband wouldn't have anything to do with it. He was more concerned with the servants on the parlor level who were anxiously waiting news of the mistress' death than he was with her cockamamie story and he as much as told her so. He said, "My dad's been dead for five years. You must have dozed off and dreamt it. We have to go downstairs." So that's what they did: they went out in the hallway and down the beautiful cantilevered stairway. She continued to tell him what she had seen, it was very important to her.

Halfway down the stairs, Margaret realized that her husband was not listening to her. His mind was on the funeral or the estate. So she fell quiet. As they reached the bottom of the stairs, the butler was standing at the front door with the doorknob in his hand and the door wide open. Tears were streaming down his face and he seemed to not notice their presence.

Mr. Gordon had to shake him. "Morrison, what's the matter?" he asked. The butler looked at them and replied, "Well, sir, I have to tell you myself, the general came in the front door and went up the stairs with his hat on his arm, looking for Miss Nellie."

Three people saw Willie that day and two lived to talk about it. It's a classic ghost story. Three people saw the same thing with no way to collaborate about it: Willie came back for his Nellie.

LADY OF THE HOUSE VISITS

As a rule, ghosts will not leave their haunt, whether it's a home or a space; usually they will not leave. Some ghosts feel at home in different areas. Evidently Mrs. Anderson is that way. She was the wife of one of the most famous Civil War generals from Savannah and she used to reside in what is today the Ballastone Inn.

The Ballastone Inn sits adjacent to the formal gardens on the east side of the Juliette Gordon Low Birthplace. It is a beautiful mansion that houses one of the finest inns in the Historic District. The Anderson family lived in this house in Miss Nellie's time and they were good acquaintances and neighbors.

Dwayne is the Innkeeper and one late afternoon he and master chef Ruby were going over the next day's breakfast menu. He was sitting at the desk in the rear of the entrance foyer and Ruby was standing over his shoulder looking at the menu. They both heard the front door open and they looked up to see a lady enter the front foyer.

Dwayne said she was an older lady about five feet tall with her gray hair pulled up in a knot on the back of her head. She wore an old fashioned dress with a bustle. Both of them said she looked like a perfectly normal old lady except that instead of walking she seemed to glide and that's when they noticed she didn't have any feet. She entered and turned into the front parlor to their left.

Dwayne got up and went forward to the door and Ruby went through the breakfast room and they both met in the parlor and found no one there. They searched the first floor and could find no one. After mentioning it to Jennifer, the owner, she told them she had met the woman who had lived in the house when it was the Lester House Hotel; Jennifer said she knew Mrs. Anderson well.

Jennifer found a photo and showed it to them. Upon seeing the picture Ruby almost fainted and Dwayne knew immediately that indeed they had seen Mrs. Anderson come home.

IN THE GLOAMING

In the gloaming, oh my darling,
When the lights are dim and low,
And the quiet shadows falling,
Softly come, and softly go.
When the winds are sobbing faintly,
With a gentle lull of woe,
Will you think of me and love me,
As you did once long ago?
In the gloaming, oh my darling,
Think not bitterly of me,
Though I passed away in silence,
Left you lonely, set you free.
For my heart was crushed with longing,
What had been could never be,
It was best to leave you thus dear,
Best for you, and best for me.

Anne F. Hamson & Meta Orred

LINDSAY-MORGAN FURNITURE STORE

The large four-story building on York Street at Wright Square has been empty for years. It was the Lindsay-Morgan Furniture Store until it closed in the 1970's and has been empty ever since. It is a prime candidate for condos, and with its great northern exposure it should be full of artists' lofts. There are about 7,000 art students in Savannah and there is a lack of housing, so this place should be full.

About five years ago, the reputation of this building as an actively haunted site got to be so bad that the owner had a certain iron plaque removed from the front of the building in order to lure interest from prospective tenants. The iron plaque explains that the building sits atop the site of Savannah's first cemetery. There were so many letters to the editor at the local newspaper that the owner was forced to put it back.

You can remove the plaque but you can't remove the burial ground.

A friend of mine sells homes in the Historic District; that's what he does and he does very well at it. Most of the Historic District—especially the business section—is condominiums. The point where I start my tours on the corner of Bull Street at York is in front of a building with retail space on the ground level and condos above. This building's condo occupancy should be full but it's empty. *It can't be rented and it can't be sold!*

My realtor friend was showing the building to a wealthy young couple from New Hampshire and they were in love with the structure. She wanted to put a studio on the second floor and live on the top floors. My friend took the couple through each floor. They got off on the top floor and he stayed by the entrance to the elevator with the husband discussing the building's features while the wife went over to the windows. The view is beautiful: one can see over the trees, the top of the monument in the square, as well as the Westin Hotel across the river—it's a wonderful view.

She got about ten feet from the windows and started screaming hysterically and wouldn't stop. The realtor was afraid to put her in the elevator because of its habit of breaking down, so they ran her downstairs to the coffee shop in the same block. They sat her down and threw some water in her face and when she became coherent, they asked her what had happened.

She said that as she approached the windows she felt very cold (even though it was a bright and sunny day in June). As soon as it got cold everything went black, and that's when she got scared. When the room went dark, a disembodied female face hovered above her near the ceiling. The face floated from side to side and then came directly toward her as if to hit her in the face. That's when she started screaming.

Needless to add, the deal was dead and the couple refused to enter that building again!

Another occurrence has to do with a shop owner named Biezenbos who has since moved from the shops on York Street. She had an art glass shop called RAF and now maintains a shop in Jacksonville, Florida. It seems she had a poltergeist that was mischievous and actually broke quite a few pieces, but she seemed content to put up with his antics; he was part of the building and she put up with him.

One day Mrs. Biezenbos was crating some objects to move to her store in Florida. It took her quite awhile to get everything wrapped and set in straw, and then she nailed the lids on the crates and loaded her van. She had an uneventful trip and arrived in front of her store on Waters Street and started to get out. She had a very bad feeling and at the same time the locks on the doors of the van would not pop open. No matter how many times she would press the button, the doors would not unlock. That's when she felt very bad; it was like an overwhelming feeling of dread. She said she immediately drove all the way back to the Savannah store and when she pulled up in front of York Street the door locks popped open and she took the last crate that she had loaded inside and the feeling went away.

Mrs. Biezenbos told me she thought she had inadvertently boxed up her poltergeist and he wanted to return to his haunt!

Wright Square is one of the four original squares laid out in 1733 by James Edward Oglethorpe. Originally called Percival Square, it was renamed in honor of the last Royal Governor, James Wright. Even though a Tory, he was an able administrator and by far the best thing to happen to this fledgling colony.

During Oglethorpe's time—just like the efficient town-plan—this was an efficient square. The courthouse stood opposite the southwest corner. The old English gaol—a one story stone and iron stockade—was located in the southwest corner adjacent to the courthouse, and in the middle of the square was the scaffold for the gallows. For the first fifteen years of this colony this was the 'hanging square'. A very efficient or vicious square if you were a criminal, from the gavel to the gallows to the grave after having left the gaol.

One noticeable feature of Wright Square is the absence of Spanish moss on the limbs of the massive live oaks. The large oaks in the southern half of the square are covered with moss while the trees in the northern half have none. Spanish moss loves oak trees but there isn't any. The moss tries to spread but it never gets a foothold. Long before I got here it was like this, and I was born and raised in Savannah.

Spanish moss just won't spread in Wright Square and some say that's because of Alice. She's up in these trees and she won't allow the Spanish moss to grow there as a sign of her presence. Alice Riley was the first woman to be hanged in Georgia, and she was hanged right there in 1735. A nineteen-year-old, blue-eyed, red haired Irish girl, she was hanged in the middle of this square for three days as a murderer and her spirit is still in this square, up in these trees.

Alice's husband was hanged eight months earlier. Both were indentured servants and conspired to murder their master, *poor old* Mr. Wise—I'm relating from the early journals of the colony, from the trial, so to speak. Having grown up in Savannah, learning how Alice and her husband murdered poor old Mr. Wise, there was no need to doubt their guilt but with research I found their master was a high member of the aristocracy with many indentured servants and he was only forty years old when they killed him, so he wasn't *poor old* Mr. Wise at all. He was a very cruel and malicious man, as well as proud and arrogant. This all came out in the trial. He had long white hair down to his belt. The aristocracy at that time mimicked the French court by wearing powdered wigs in public. So all Mr. Wise had to do was pile his white hair on top of his head and he was in high fashion.

Alice was a close member of Mr. Wise's household staff, and one of their rituals was that Alice would wash his hair. Once or twice a week he would hang his head out of his bed and she would wash his hair in a bucket. After some cruel and malicious behavior on his part, Alice and her husband held his head in the bucket, and they drowned him.

The couple escaped to Isle of Hope, an old frontier outpost then, and a beautiful residential area today. They were caught after two days, brought back and put on trial. In a trial by peers, you stood for yourself or had a fellow colonist stand for you. Even though mitigating circumstances due to Mr. Wise's cruel and malicious behavior came out in the trial, it was a case of premeditated murder. Alice and her husband were guilty and were both sentenced to death.

Upon sentencing, the whole courthouse went out into the square and watched as the authorities hanged Alice's common law husband, Richard White. He was left to twist in the wind for three days. However, the court had to wait eight months to hang Alice because she was with child. So—as we would do today—she had the baby, but they put her in the stockade to do so, which is not a very good place to have a child, in the gaol.

Surprisingly, Alice had the baby and it was put up for adoption. Then the court had to hang Alice, but they didn't want to hang her. The colony was less than three years old and had never hanged a woman before; only three men prior, one of which was her husband, and they didn't want a woman hanging in the middle of Wright Square for three days. But they had to do it. So they came up with a plan to double the height of the scaffold and made the gallows twice as tall to hang her high. Walking through the square, rubbernecks had to look for Alice up in the trees.

And that's why there's no Spanish moss in those trees today because Alice is up there, looking for her baby. The baby only made it forty-five days and died of pneumonia.

The guilty were hanged for three days, primarily for two reasons. The first was as a deterrent. That's the theory anyway. Someone is going to think twice before committing a heinous crime if they remember bodies hanging there for three days. The other reason was to make sure the condemned was deceased.

Georgia was an English colony and to be hanged by the neck until dead is an English form of execution—a very mild form of execution by English standards of the day, for the Brits had many more colorful ways of putting the condemned to death. Look at William Wallace, Brave-heart, for instance; parts of him were spread all over the realm.

Pirates in particular would abhor being measured for the gibbets (iron suits custom made to insure one could not be buried) before they were to be hanged. After the sea rovers were taken down their bodies were tarred and locked in the gibbets to hang at the mouth of the harbor as a warning to other sailors not to turn to piracy. The bodies were tarred so that they would last longer in the weather and the gibbets insured that any crew or family member couldn't give them a Christian burial. So the bodies would hang out there until they were sun dried and the bones picked clean by birds.

CHATHAM SQUARE EXORCISM

A small row of townhouses face Chatham Square on the west and each are single dwellings. One of the structures in the row is owned by a couple who rent it out nightly as an overflow for their bed & breakfast and it is furnished with all the amenities of a well-stocked home. I have always had brochures for my ghost tour in their B&B, and one day I ran into one of the owners. She informed me that she had removed all the rack cards that had anything to do with the supernatural.

I asked why and was told that an exorcism had been performed at the residence and she didn't want any more spectral activity. When pressed for a reason, she informed me that, after a series of phenomena had occurred, the house had to be blessed and cleansed of spectral activity and she didn't want a return of the ghosts. A local Episcopalian priest had cleansed the house and she was afraid of enticing them back.

It seems that over a period of months the housekeepers were having trouble in the townhouse and wouldn't stay to finish their work. Some said they felt a presence in the house and wouldn't go back in alone. One in particular said that there was a man who would follow her from one room to the next, and when she confronted him, he disappeared. She told her employers that she would not go back in the house alone.

One evening a couple phoned at 2 a.m. and said they wanted another place to stay and would the innkeeper please come and move them. The innkeeper drove over in the mini van to pick up the guests and found them on the stoop outside with their bags packed. They would not speak of what happened but insisted they be brought to another location to continue their stay. It was thought that maybe they were just shook up because they had taken one of my walking ghost tours that very night and the owners chalked it up as just an overworked imagination.

A second couple called to say that they wanted their money back. They would be leaving the city that morning even though they had booked the townhouse for an entire week and had only spent one night. The story they told is fascinating. The first night the woman went to bed about 10 p.m. while her husband stayed up answering e-mails, and about 10:30 p.m. he followed his wife upstairs. He put on his pajamas and got in bed with her. He said he was tired and it didn't take him moments to fall asleep.

He awoke to find himself on the floor next to the bed. He got on his knees and looked at his wife and found her sound asleep. He got up and got back in bed. He said it took him about ten to fifteen minutes to fall back to sleep. He said he rolled over only to find himself on the floor. He lay there and thought to himself, "I've only had two glasses of wine and I've never fallen out of bed before." That's what he thought. He had fallen out of the bed. He wasn't thinking paranormal here. He just thought he had fallen out of the bed, twice!

He said he got up the third time and crawled in bed next to his wife, who was still sound asleep. It took him a while to doze off this time, about twenty to thirty minutes. He said he was sound asleep and woke to find himself lying on the floor next to the bed. He said he wasn't getting back in that bed, so he slept in a chair. The next morning his wife awoke to find her husband sleeping in the large comfortable chair by the window.

The way it was told to me, she wanted to know why he was sleeping in the chair. They were standing next to the brick wall in the upstairs bedroom and he was explaining why, when *something picked him up and threw him against the wall!* They both packed their bags and called a cab. They left the city that morning.

After such harrowing experiences, the owners asked their parish priest to come and check the house. I talked to a priest at the cathedral and he told me the same thing that the innkeeper's parish priest had said: "When a parishioner calls you up like that, you very politely bring the crucifix, the Bible and some holy water and you go and bless the house. You walk through and bless the furniture, you bless the rooms and then you go outside and bless the house. That usually makes everyone happy unless you feel something." And that is exactly what their clergyman said: he said when he walked in the front door he felt a palpable presence. It felt very overwhelming and seemed to weigh down on him in a heavy manner. I asked him what he felt and he said it was a malevolent being.

It took him about four weeks to get permission from the Diocese in Macon to perform an exorcism. The owner went through the house with him. They were on the first floor and he read the rites and spread the holy water. Exorcism is performed by Catholic, Presbyterian and Episcopalian clergy and it is very specific. One reads the rites as put down in the prayer book.

The innkeeper said that the priest read the part about evil hauntings and spread the holy water and nothing happened. They went upstairs to the bedroom and he read the part about ghosts and told the ghost to move on, that "Christ had heaven open for him and he should move on." She said when he read that part you could feel a cold blast of air in the middle of the room and the specter presumably left.

Neither the ghost or my ghost tour brochures have returned to the premises.

SLIMED

I met a couple from Atlanta who had come to Savannah for the summer and were staying in a rental house on one of the squares. Wiley and Janet were interested in moving to Savannah and were looking for somewhere to buy in the Historic District. Being fans of barbeque, we all got along famously and spent some time together swapping ghost stories. Janet related to me a sequence of events that are fantastic, to say the least.

While making the bed one morning, she heard pacing on the wood floor above the master bedroom. She heard it several times more, usually in the daytime; five paces in one direction, and then back and forth. It sounded like a woman with high-heeled boots.

They called the absentee owner to ask if anyone should be upstairs and he said no. There was no way upstairs except through the front door. The owner told them to call the police, but they didn't. Instead, they took a large chair that was in the front hall and slid it in front of the door. If someone were upstairs, they would have to move it to get out. Janet also put some invisible tape on a couple of spots on the door. Neither the chair nor the tape was ever moved. The TV and radio turned on and off several times, seemingly by themselves.

The cleaning lady was in their apartment and needed a mop from the upstairs unit. Janet told the maid that they had seen the light upstairs and thinking someone had been up there, they put the big up-holstered chair in front of the door. Therefore, the maid would have to use the door inside to go upstairs. When Janet told her about the light, the maid said that she had heard footsteps in the past and remembered other strange things had happened, like the upstairs tub filling with water.

They were both now freaked out, yet the maid still needed the mop, so the ladies went upstairs together and got the mop. Everything looked ok. Returning to the apartment, Janet's dog Radar became agitated in the middle of the living room and pulled Janet into the kitchen and then towards where the maid's helper was working. Janet's biggest fear was that Radar (being a 125 lb. German Shepherd) would attack the helper. Instead, he dragged Janet into the bedroom and charged to the back corner of the room. His hackles were up and he was barking ferociously as if someone were standing up on the bed in the corner of the room. Janet had to literally drag him out of the room.

While dining out one afternoon, Wiley received a phone call on his cell. No one responded, so Wiley called the number back and left a message that he was trying to return the call. When he returned home, the message light was blinking. He had never given that phone number to anyone, so he was curious and played the message: it was Wiley's voice and message about returning the phone call.

One day Janet was listening to her radio while she ironed and picked up the house. She remembers shutting the radio off before going to bed that night, but awoke in the middle of the night to a humming noise and figured one of the ceiling fans was having trouble. She got to the doorway of the living room and noticed the fans were not spinning, so she went to investigate the noise. It was emanating from the radio. She could not turn it off.

At that point she noticed two things: one, there was a gooey, sticky substance all over the buttons; two, there was liquid underneath the radio. There was no water source from above. Janet had to unplug the radio to stop the noise. She then sopped up the liquid. It was colorless and odorless and it took about three or four paper towels to absorb all the liquid.

Janet tried to wipe up the gooey mess, but a lot of it remained. She went back to bed. The next morning she asked Wiley if he had done anything to the radio, and he had no idea what she was talking about. The only reason they could come up with was that their radio had been slimed!

THE ANCHORAGE

I couldn't do this tour if I didn't believe in ghosts. One experience that made me a believer happened when I was a boat captain working in the Gulf of Mexico. I used to run jack-up rigs; these are vessels with three legs that jack up and down to make moveable platforms. This particular vessel had 135-foot legs and a large deck for construction equipment and a very large cabin to accommodate work crews.

We were traveling from the port of New Orleans to Galveston Bay on our way to another job location and had no work crew and an empty deck. The vessel had a complement of five crewmen, a captain, mate, cook, deck hand and an engineer. We had been traveling for some twenty hours and had arrived in the wee hours of the morning a day ahead of schedule. Instead of going into port and having my crew disappear into one of the many dens of iniquity in the port of Galveston, I decided to stay offshore and set up in the anchorage just to the east of the ship channel.

It was one or two in the morning and the crew was asleep except for the deck hand and myself. I jacked the vessel up in the area designated on the chart as a safe haven. I told the deck hand to get some sleep and I shut down the main engines with only the generator left running. I went below, laid down in my bunk and fell fast asleep.

The strange feeling of being strangled awakened me. I couldn't breathe. I distinctly felt what seemed like two strong hands grasped around my neck and I couldn't catch my breath. I forced myself up out of the bunk and ran into the cook's cabin. I tried to rouse him but I couldn't speak. I just stood there and watched as he slept fitfully.

The whole time this horrible feeling of doom was all about me; a feeling of helplessness and despair. It is very hard to explain, the only other time I felt such a sensation was visiting Shiloh battlefield at the sunken road of the 'Hornet's Nest,' when I got this terrible feeling of anxiety that only lifted when I walked ten to fifteen yards away from the site.

I ran into the mate's cabin and experienced the same problem. No matter what I did, I couldn't wake him. I immediately went to the wheelhouse and cranked the main engines. As soon as they began to idle properly, I started to jack the vessel down into the water and the moment the legs began to lift free from the surface of the sea floor, the feeling went away. No more heavy feeling of dread and gloom, it was as if a load had been lifted from my shoulders and my spirits began to lift.

I steered the boat to the west side of the channel, set the legs down and jacked the rig up out of the water. I was physically drained and covered in sweat. I went to my cabin, fell in my bunk and went to sleep. Later that day I told the cook what had happened, he looked at me as if I were kidding and said I must have had a nightmare, but I was not pulling his leg. The whole episode was too real to be a dream. As far as I have been able to work it out in my mind, this is what

HAUNTINGS!

I have determined to be the cause of my distress: we had set down on a shipwreck, a sunken vessel of dead souls who had no desire to have their rest disturbed. It could have been a vessel sunk in a storm or one of the pirate vessels sunk in a battle off the port of Galveston. In order to make me move, I was attacked by a specter who did not want me there. Since I was the captain of the boat, the apparition forced me to take action. I will never forget that episode and it gave me a real sense of the other side and a respect for a burial place, whether it is on land or sea!

BONAVENTURE CEMETERY

Cemeteries have always been promenades, places for strolls and visits in the Victorian tradition. It is an age-old custom to visit with the deceased and you will notice that the tombs are often situated with a parlor or yard like setting in front or to the side with cast iron furniture for seating.

Bonaventure was converted to a cemetery before the Civil War. Formerly a plantation, the cemetery is typical of the Victorian period. With the rise of the middle class in the latter part of the 19th century, America's thoughts and ideas about death began to change. Death became romanticized and was often referred to as sleep. Elaborate grave markers and lush landscapes began to prevail. Even epitaphs reflected this change, often referring to the deceased as in 'silent slumber' or 'sweet repose'. The overall atmosphere in Victorian cemeteries is one of hope.

Mourning became more ritualized during this period. Strict guidelines were developed; regulations governed every aspect of mourner's lives from their clothing and accessories to their actions. The deceased could be put on display longer with the development of embalming practices as well as the development of a separate profession to deal with the burial preparations. The creation of funeral parlors meant the deceased were in mortuaries rather than in private homes as they had been before. This shielded the family from the gruesome task of handling the body after death.

People became separated from the morbid realities of death. They went to cemeteries for Sunday strolls and family picnics. Visits to cemeteries were no longer dreaded events. An ideal southern Victorian cemetery, there is much of Savannah's and Georgia's history buried at Bonaventure. Created in 1846 on what was originally the site of the Mullryne and Tattnall plantation, Bonaventure means "Good Fortune."

In 1760, Colonel John Mullryne and his son-in-law Josiah Tattnall, both of Beaufort, South Carolina, settled on adjoining land on St. Augustine Creek, now part of the Wilmington River. The oak trees and avenues are laid out in the shape of the letters M & T to commemorate the marriage of the two families.

The two men were loyalists and even helped the Royal governor, James Wright, escape aboard the HMS Scarborough to England. Mullryne fled to the Bahamas and Tattnall to England. The property was confiscated and sold to John Habersham at auction in 1782. Josiah Tatnall, Jr. returned from England when he was 18 years old to fight under Continental Army General Nathaniel Greene and Mad Anthony Wayne, thereby recovering his father's estate in 1785. He introduced a new strain of long staple cotton from the Bahamas to Bonaventure.

He married Harriet Fenwicke in 1786, and was elected Governor of Georgia in 1801. His wife died in 1802, and is buried at Bonaventure alongside some of their children who died in infancy. He died in the Bahamas in 1803, and is buried alongside his wife. The surviving children were sent to live in England with their grandfather.

Josiah Tattnall III outlived his siblings and became sole owner of Bonaventure in 1832. He had returned to America and joined the U.S. Navy in 1812. He had a distinguished career and fought in the Mexican War in the 1840's. Once Tattnall breached America's neutrality by aiding the British fleet fighting in Chinese waters. His remark when reprimanded was, "Blood is thicker than water." He resigned in 1861 to serve as Commodore of the Confederate States Navy. He died in Savannah in 1871 and was buried with his family.

The plantation's main house burned one evening during a dinner party. The fire started in the roof and by the time it was noticed the mansion could not be saved. Rather than disrupt his guests Commodore Tattnall had the furniture moved outside and the party continued by the warm light of the burning house. After dinner the guests joined the Commodore in a toast after which he broke his crystal goblet against a massive oak tree and to this day people can still hear the shattering of glass.

One night not long ago a group of yachtsmen from Hilton Head Island was traveling the Inter-coastal Waterway and saw figures in period dress moving about amid music and candlelight. They called and found out the cemetery closes at five p.m. and there had been no special function the night before.

Since Commodore Tattnall lived most of his life at sea, he rarely spent time at the plantation and in 1846 he sold 160 acres to Peter Wiltberger, owner of the Pulaski House Hotel, for five thousand dollars. That excluded the house grounds and family burial plot but Wiltberger agreed to maintain it. He planned to turn the estate into a cemetery. However, he died in 1853 and is buried with his wife and son at Bonaventure.

His other son, Major William Wiltberger inherited the plantation. During the Civil War he was Captain of Company B of the Georgia Hussars and became a Major in 1864. After the war he operated the Pulaski House Hotel and in 1858 he formed the Evergreen Cemetery Company. He died in 1872 and is buried with his family in section B, lot 3. After his death, the City of Savannah bought the cemetery from his estate for $30,000.00.

To list the many notable people buried in Bonaventure would take a book in and of itself, but I will name a few with a brief history of each. The oldest burial at the cemetery is William Butler. He died in 1761 and was buried at Silk Hope, a plantation he established in 1755, and was reintered in Bonaventure in 1858. He was tax collector and surveyor of highways. His obituary spoke of his 'amiable qualities' and 'benevolent disposition'. He is said to be seen sitting on his marker and will speak to passers-by in the daytime hours; his first grave was disturbed, after all.

Upon entering Bonaventure the first vault you see is that of William Gaston, it was originally at the entrance to Colonial Cemetery. A respected Savannah merchant, he was well known for his hospitality and kindness to strangers. He died in New York City and upon his death, Savannahians took up a subscription to build his vault. It was designed as a temporary resting place for the bodies of strangers who died in the city. Mayor Thomas Gamble wrote in 1925 that Gaston was "host to the living and the dead."

The Savannah Police, the Georgia Hussars, the Knights Templar and the Hibernian Society erected one of the most imposing monuments for Robert Houston Anderson. He graduated from West Point in 1857, resigned from the U.S. Army in 1861, became a brigadier general in the Confederate Army, and was Chief of Police from 1866-1888. He haunts the police barracks at Oglethorpe and Habersham Streets.

Another citizen of note, Dr. Richard Arnold was a prominent physician and mayor of the city when it surrendered to Federal forces in 1864. He helped found the American Medical Association and the Georgia Historical Society. He is heard to walk the halls of old Candler Hospital, the site of the Georgia Medical College, which he started after the yellow fever epidemic of 1854.

Resting alone in section E, lot 99 is Gracie Watson. She haunts the northwest corner of Bull and Bryan Streets at the site of the Pulaski House Hotel (now a bank). Many people see Gracie to this day and hers is one of the most sought after graves at Bonaventure. Gracie was the only child of W. J. and Frances Watson, who managed the hotel for Peter Wiltberger. She was known for her sweetness and was a favorite of hotel guests. She contracted pneumonia at the age of six and died two days after Easter in 1889. Her funeral was held in the lobby of the hotel. The next year the Watsons left the Pulaski House, as Mr. Watson became the manager of the new Desoto Hotel.

In 1890, Watson handed a photograph of his daughter to John Walz, master sculptor. Carved of white Georgia marble, hers is a chillingly lifelike image and is said by many to glow in the light of the moon. She is alone, as her parents left Savannah and she is the only person buried in the lot. Her appeal is in the realism of the statue and the soft serene vision of her face. Gifts are often left: shiny pennies or small presents at Christmas time.

Solomon Gleason produced much of the decorative ironwork throughout Savannah as well as Laurel Grove and Bonaventure cemeteries at his foundry and the prominent Irish founders apprenticed under him. Buried next to his family, he wrote in his diary of often visiting his beloved son and wife in Bonaventure. He died in the yellow fever epidemic of 1876.

Edward Telfair was Governor of Georgia in 1786 and his son was State Representative and later U.S. Congressman. Mary and Margaret Telfair, daughters of Edward and Sarah Telfair, erected the monument. The last of her line, Mary inherited the family home on Telfair Square and bequeathed the house to become the first art museum in the South. She also founded the Telfair Infirmary for women and a home for widows.

Mary is known to haunt the Telfair Museum of Art and the Georgia Historical Society reading room, both of which she donated. In her will it stated that the family name would remain prominent and that no public speaking or cocktail parties would be held in either building. You can't attract members or run a successful museum without lectures and alcoholic beverages, so the establishments to this day are distracted by mysterious loud noises and numerous broken bottles at the bar during receptions and galas.

John Walz was born in Stuttgart, Germany, and is the most recognized sculptor in Savannah. He came to the city to carve the statues in front of the Telfair Museum of Art and fell in love with the area. Well known for funerary monuments, his work is found in Bonaventure, Laurel Grove, and Catholic cemeteries with over 70 works in Bonaventure alone. Alas, there is no headstone on his grave.

Peter Meldrim purchased the home of Charles Green on Madison Square after the Civil War and his family lived in the home until 1943. It is now the Parish House for St. John's Episcopal Church. He is the father of Sophie Meldrim, said to have been the most beautiful woman the South ever produced and she is buried next to her parents.

John Mongin's beautiful Egyptian pyramid sits overlooking the bluff in one of the choicest spots in the graveyard. In 1873, his family vault was dismantled and moved here from Daufuskie Island where he had extensive land holdings. They were one of many families to relocate their dead to Bonaventure. He operated the first steamship between Savannah and Charleston. In 1989 the vault was vandalized and the remains were stolen.

CSA Brigadier General Alexander R. Lawton was originally buried in Laurel Grove Cemetery with his daughter Corrine, who died at the age of 31, but their remains were moved in 1878 to the bluff overlooking the Wilmington River. Lawton became Quartermaster of the Confederacy after being wounded at Sharpsburg. Their home stands on Chippewa Square and Corrine died in that house. She is seen quite often in the hallways and on the stairs of the house. His monument and the very life-like statue of his daughter were sculpted in Florence, Italy.

Johnny Mercer, co-founder of Capital Records, is buried alongside his wife Ginger. He was the most popular songwriter of the 20th Century; he wrote over 1500 songs and won 4 Academy Awards. He grew up on Vernon View and the stretch of river he lived on was renamed Moon River in his honor. His epitaph is "and the Angels sing," and his wife's reads, "You must have been a beautiful baby."

Conrad Aiken grew up at 230 South Broad Street (today Oglethorpe Avenue) and at the age of nine his parents were involved in a murder/suicide. The father killed the mother and then himself. Conrad ran across the street to the Police Barracks and the officer on duty wrote about the courage of the young boy as he showed the men the bodies. He was raised by relatives in Boston and went to Harvard. He became a Pulitzer winning poet and National Book Award author and he and his wife lived in London, New York and Boston. Upon retiring and returning to Savannah, they bought the house next door at 228 E.

Oglethorpe. Conrad died in 1973 and his wife passed away in 1992. They were famous for their hospitality and had a party at least once a month. She was famous for her martinis.

Unlike most people who go to parks or sit on the waterfront to unwind, the Aikens would go to Bonaventure, where one of their favorite things to do was sit at his parents' gravesite and drink martinis. One day they were sitting on the bluff having drinks when Conrad remarked, "Damn, there is no more ice!" His wife said about three minutes later it started hailing. We know from his will that Conrad didn't want a tombstone or a monument; he wanted a bench. When you go to Bonaventure, you can see this bench. It is inscribed with Aiken's name. He had the bench put there so his friends could come and sit and have a drink with him. I have seen people drinking martinis and I've even seen some pour good gin right on his grave.

Near the end of his life Conrad and his wife were sitting on the bluff watching the ships on the Savannah River and he noticed one called the *Cosmos Mariner.* Checking the Savannah newspaper for the shipping news, Aiken discovered that the *Cosmos Mariner* was headed for a "Destination Unknown," and he liked it so much, he used "Cosmos Mariner, Destination Unknown" as his epitaph.

ROOT

'Some folks can wuk roots. Dey had duh
powuh to lay down sumpm tuh harm
yuh.'
'Conjuh is magic some folks is bawn wid, it
gibs um powuh obuh things udduh folks
dohn uddastan.'
Drums and Shadows

'I was birthed with my wisdom because I
was the seventh child and baun with a
'caul', I kin see um cuz uh wuz bawn wid
a doubul caul and fut foemos.'
'Dat gib yuh duh powuh to see um.'

Fifty Years as a Lowcountry Witch-Doctor
Conjure or Spells, "Conjuh"

Introduced by African slaves who had practiced
magic for thousands of years long before doctors as
we know them, witch doctors are medicine men who
live close to nature and utilize roots and herbs to treat
the afflicted. They obtain their knowledge secretly by
inheritance. They commune with the spirits of the night
who help them cure or curse those who come to their
attention. When the moon is full, or in its sickle shape,
is the period when spells are more potent. The doctor
needs a lock of hair or fingernail paring, but a photo
or a piece of clothing will do. One must be sure that
the person the hex is placed on is aware that he, or

she, has been hexed. The hex client has been put at ease. He has seen the doctor working with his dolls, herbs and magic powders to make the charms. He has heard him speak in an unknown language and perform mystic rites. African witch doctors (predominant in this area) assume the name of the bird or beast from whom they obtain their power and the men are supreme.

In Louisiana, Mississippi, and Alabama women are the dominant leaders in voodoo (a different form of magic.) Snake worship, animal sacrifice, blood drinking, and gris gris (African amulet) combine to form a cult centered around dancing and drumming used to build up erotic and frenzied passions.

White America clings to European witchcraft with its covens, Satanism, and fertility rites as well as its witches and warlocks. It is an occult filling its pockets from the gullible. African witchcraft has not changed over the years and root doctors avoid rather than seek publicity—no groups or covens, just individual doctors, witch doctors.

In nights only recently past, the throb of drums echoed from the marsh, announcing the black art known as root—forces of the night. Magical potions, astral spirits, hexes, spells used by the witch doctor, or root doctor, used to perform white and black magic permeated the air. Speaking in the 'unknown tongue' a hex doll or a death root was empowered; a finger nail clipping or lock of hair sewn inside a flannel hex doll with pins through the part where you want the victim to feel pain.

A root buried in the yard will cause pain in the legs and also cause the garden to die. Another root doctor must be brought in for a cure. A person puts "the mouth on you" and you will have bad trouble unless you hire a doctor to "chew the root". Toenails, fingernail clippings, even the scrapings from the bottom of the foot, are all very powerful when mixed with whiskey.

African witchcraft on plantations during the full moon, or sickle phase, would have the drums beating and all the slaves knew the spirit of darkness was coming. Evil cannot pass the color blue; evil spirits shun the color blue so all openings of homes were painted blue, hence the term "haint blue". Juju, root, hex, the root doctor dictated spirits of the night, potions and taboos. His word was law to his patients; he was omnipotent. Witch doctors described what and when to plant, and they exorcised evil spirits.

Doctor Buzzard of local fame was a direct descendant of an African witch doctor, and then there was a Doctor Crow, Dr. Bug, Dr. Hawk, and Dr. Snake. Held in prison on the west coast of Africa after having failed in predictions to the chief of his tribe that lost in battle, Doctor Buzzard was sold to America as a slave. Plantation owners did not want witch doctors and usually let them flee to the outskirts in the marginal swamps and marshes.

Dr. Bug mixed arsenic with moonshine to produce heart palpitations to beat the draft for his clients during the Vietnam War. He would dip his penknife in the arsenic and stir the shot of moonshine before administrating to his 'patient'.

These doctors could put a spell on or take a spell off. They talked with spirits in the unknown tongue, and made roots and potions for charms with spells, powders, chew the root, spirits, and parts of owls, frogs, snakes, etc.; salamanders were especially prized.

Dirt from a preacher's grave will take a spell off, but dirt from a criminal's grave is used for sickness and death roots. Hex roots, blue flannel and red flannel amulets were prepared with the utmost care. The witch doctor must ascertain the astral force, then by invocation he calls in the proper kinetic force to place in the amulet. Some amulets are prepared in advance for common cases and to get immediate results. Peace of mind, luck, and love are always red flannel. Herbs, roots of plants and bone are used. Blue flannel is used when evil is involved.

A witch doctor's amulet is his trademark. The shape is always the same, and the color changes with the application. Hex roots or amulets are different from mass produced 'prayer cloths' sold by healers. White witchcraft is used by certain doctors to free people from evil forces and protect victims from black witchcraft; white is stronger than black. Black witchcraft is when someone in the occult field uses a death root or black root to cause ruin, sickness, and misfortune. A witch doctor who performs both white and black magic has less power because he has to obey two masters. Serving two is hard in the physical plane but in the astral it is much more difficult.

A FEW LAST THOUGHTS

Guests joining me for a See Savannah Walking Tour often ask me if after all my encounters with the supernatural whether I'm afraid of ghosts. To be perfectly honest, no, for the more I find out about hauntings and what causes them the less I am afraid of death. If there is any truth to these accounts then all it seems to indicate to me is that there is no end to life, and I think of that as a good thing, not a bad thing. For much of my life I had serious doubts whether there is life after death, or if there is a heaven and hell and if so, how does it operate and where. The existence of ghosts tends to prove that there is an experience beyond the grave, whether you want to call it life after death, reincarnation, or whatever.

Of course, I have no intention of coming back as a ghost. Most ghosts seem to be terribly unhappy, caught between here and the next world with no ability to take care of unfinished business. Eventually they fade away, for it's a matter of physics not faith that spirit energy unsupported by the human body cannot sustain itself and gradually disperses. Where it goes and what it does next, I'm not sure.

One thing is for certain, though. The past is not restricted to the past in Savannah. It continues to evolve on some level of existence, perhaps in another dimension. And the past has a remarkable habit of breaking through into the present, in the weirdest ways and in the strangest places, at the oddest times.

Then, too, maybe ghosts aren't such tragic figures on second thought. After all, I can't think of a better place than Savannah to spend eternity.

Maybe this is heaven.

SEE SAVANNAH WALKING TOURS:

Savannah Saunter: History, Gardens and Architecture - 10 a.m. and 2 p.m. daily

Homemade Thunder: Civil War Walk - daily 10 a.m.

Pirate's Walk: True Tales of Treasure & Sea Rovers of Yesteryear. Daily at 2 p.m. and 4 p.m. Departs from Blackbeard's Toy Store at #1 Lincoln Street Ramp (Lincoln and River Streets.)

Hauntings Tour: Legendary Locations and Eyewitness Accounts of the Paranormal. Daily at 7 p.m. and 9 p.m. Tours depart from Urban Cargo Gift Shop at 135 Bull Street (corner of Bull & York on Wright Square.)

For information: (912) 441-9277